It's Never Been Easier to Hire the Wrong Attorney

It's Never Been Easier to Hire the Wrong Attorney

DAVID W. CRAIG

AUTHOR OF *SEMITRUCK WRECK: A GUIDE FOR VICTIMS AND THEIR FAMILIES*

with ABIGAIL HAYS

HOUNDSTOOTH
PRESS

IT'S NEVER BEEN EASIER TO HIRE THE WRONG ATTORNEY

FIRST EDITION

ISBN   978-1-5445-4765-7   *Hardcover*
         978-1-5445-4764-0   *Paperback*
         978-1-5445-4766-4   *Ebook*
         978-1-5445-4767-1   *Audiobook*

Contents

NOTE TO READER 9

INTRODUCTION...11

1. THEY'RE EVERYWHERE 17

2. HOW DID WE GET HERE? 23

3. THE PROBLEM.. 33

4. PICKING THE WRONG ATTORNEY 37

5. PICKING THE RIGHT ATTORNEY....................... 65

CONCLUSION.. 87

APPENDIX I 89

APPENDIX II 99

ABOUT THE AUTHORS..101

Note to Reader

IF YOU NEED AN ATTORNEY, YOU NEED TO UNDERSTAND that picking the wrong attorney can be devastating and have long-lasting ramifications.

This book is written to help you avoid making that mistake. This doesn't mean that picking the right attorney will be easy. In fact, it is easier to pick the wrong attorney than the right one. Elements like billboards, Google Ads, and TV commercials can, unfortunately, sway people into thinking that the number of advertisements is equal to the level of expertise of the attorney. This is simply not true. Inside this book, you will find an explanation of the history of legal advertising, discussion about various types of advertising methods used today and the ethics of legal advertising, real-life examples of the consequences of inadequate legal representation, and best practices to select the right attorney for your legal matter.

If you read this book and follow its guidance, putting in the work, you should be on the right track. The bigger the legal challenges you face, the more important it is to follow this book's guidance in selecting your attorney.

DISCLAIMER

As a disclaimer, there are excellent attorneys who do not have the qualifications or associations or otherwise meet the criteria that I outline. These attorneys are perfectly capable of doing an excellent job for you. There are also attorneys who may meet the criteria that I have outlined who are not a good fit or may not be the best attorney for your legal matter. The problem is, as a nonattorney, trying to figure out who is good and who isn't as good is difficult, if not impossible. By following the guidelines outlined in this book, you will significantly increase the likelihood of picking the right attorney.

Introduction

WHY WRITE THIS BOOK? THE SIMPLE ANSWER IS THAT I have seen the harm caused by people picking the wrong attorney.

It is painful to witness. I saw a case where a semi–tractor trailer backed into a young man, causing him catastrophic injuries. He was paralyzed, wouldn't be able to work again, and would need twenty-four-hour care every day for the rest of his life. Once he got out of the rehab hospital, his brother took care of him. His brother was a caring person who was worried about the future. He was the one who was tasked with finding an attorney. The semitruck was owned by a huge corporation that was making billions and had multiple layers of insurance with over $100 million in coverage. The brother was a hardworking and intelligent person who worked as a laborer. He knew no attorneys. He had no idea how to hire an attorney or what to look for in an attorney.

The brother called a personal injury attorney in the state where the injuries occurred. The injured brother had been moved out of the state to his brother's house. The brother called the attorney and told him the facts and said he was wondering if he needed to hire an attorney. He also had questions about how he could get immediate help. Financially, they were struggling to purchase their medical and daily needs. They didn't have savings or anywhere to turn. They had lots of questions. All questions were financial in nature and about how long it would take for this matter to be resolved. This attorney tried for several weeks to reassure the brother, answer his questions, and be hired as the attorney. Everything was done over the telephone because they were states away from each other.

At the same time the personal injury attorney was talking to this potential client, the trucking company was pulling together a plan to protect itself and minimize the cost of their truck driver's mistake. They put together a team. The team consisted of one of the most charismatic and convincing large claim representatives they had in the company. The truck company then sent that person to the town where the brothers were living. This claim representative went to meet the brother in person. He brought them food and told them how sorry the company was for what had happened and that the company had sent him personally to be sure all their current and future needs were met. The claim representative was able to convince the brother that they didn't need to hire an attorney who would take one-third of the settlement. Instead, they could deal directly with him and cut out the middleman. The case settled for $2 million. At the time, the case was worth more than $75 million.

Obviously, the clients would have been far better off settling for $75 million or more, even after the cost of an attorney. Two million dollars seemed like a lot of money to the brothers—and it is. However, it isn't even enough to pay for the man's past and future medical needs. Unfortunately, I was called after it was too late. The attorney had finally decided to reach out to a truck accident attorney for help, but it was too late. This situation struck me. What a huge and life-altering mistake had been made by talking to an attorney who wasn't familiar with these types of cases and had no idea how to protect the client.

Any qualified truck accident attorney would have immediately flown to the city where the brother lived. They would have warned them about the trucking company, its insurance company, and their claims people. They would have discussed the future care costs and the need for an adequate and fair settlement. They would have helped them figure out how to financially get by and take care of their needs while the case was pending. Because they spoke with the wrong attorney, they were unprepared, uninformed, and fell for the quick-money promise (the check was written and delivered with the release of all claims). Within a couple of days of meeting with the claim representative, the clients lost out on millions of dollars. What is worse is that the man's quality of life will be significantly worse because he won't have the money he needs for his future.

I have seen the harm in other areas of law as well. I have seen one person hire a good divorce attorney and the other spouse hire one that is not as skilled. I have seen results that are devastating to the spouse, both in the division of property, but also with custody and visitation rights. I have seen cases where the divorce involved more money and complicated financial dealings than the attorney was prepared to deal with. The attorney didn't know which experts to hire. As a result, I saw a case where a wife got far less than she would have gotten if she had chosen the right attorney.

I have also seen the consequence where a person charged with a crime hired the wrong attorney. They ended up being convicted and serving more jail time than another facing similar charges, but who had hired the right attorney. Not all criminal attorneys are the same, and unfortunately, the wrong attorney can cause unfair and unjust results.

People I know regularly ask me for advice on hiring attorneys for a variety of legal needs in areas of law that I don't handle. However, I certainly know how to pick the right attorneys. I regularly give out names of attorneys who can help people. I have even directed people away from attorneys who are not the right fit for a particular case. Just like the top doctors and surgeons know who the other top doctors and surgeons are, attorneys know the same. However, not everyone has access to a top attorney to advise them on whom to hire. That is why I wrote this book. My goal is for you to understand how to do the research necessary to pick the right attorney: where to look, where not to look, and how to avoid the pitfalls that might lead you in the wrong direction. My hope and desire is to teach people how to make informed decisions when it comes to choosing the right attorney to represent them. I desire that people know how to identify whether an attorney is qualified to handle their case. I want them to be able to make wise choices so they have the best chance to get what they deserve for themselves and their family. Additionally, for the sake of this book, it is also important to note that words like "picking," "choosing," "hiring," and "retaining" are all used interchangeably when it comes to selecting the right attorney for your legal matter.

My last book, *Semitruck Wreck: A Guide for Victims and Their Families* (available on Amazon), has been read by thousands of people all over the country. I realized that even though I won't meet or be hired by all these people, I have helped them by writing the book. My goal is the same with this book.

CHAPTER 1

They're Everywhere

PICKING AN ATTORNEY HAS NEVER BEEN EASIER. THEY ARE everywhere. In 2024, there were over 1.3 million attorneys in the United States to select from.[1] You can't watch TV or listen to the radio without seeing or hearing an ad from an attorney or law firm. Some attorneys pay a premium so that when you listen to the radio in your car, their name is displayed on your car's radio display, or even on your digital driver's screen. You can't drive very far without seeing an attorney's billboards. If you attend a professional, college, or even high school sports event, you are likely to encounter attorney advertising. If you live in a larger city, you will see attorney advertising on the sides of buses, trains, or subways. There are attorney display ads at the airports and on taxicabs. In some cities, rideshare vehicles are wrapped with a law firm ad. It is possible for a law firm to have many of their wrapped vehicles show up at events where large numbers of people attend. I have even seen

---

[1] Sharon Mikki, "Lawyer Statistics for Success in 2025," *Clio* (blog), last updated January 10, 2025, https://www.clio.com/blog/lawyer-statistics/.

attorneys display ads in public restrooms. Attorneys advertise in newspapers, business journals, and magazines. Many local Little Leagues, community festivals, and other events are sponsored by attorneys or they have their names clearly displayed. Those few phone books that still exist are typically dominated by attorney ads.

Between 2017 and 2021, approximately $6.8 billion was spent on advertising by law firms in the United States.[2] It was estimated that over $8.4 billion would be spent by attorneys, law firms, and businesses in legal service areas in 2024.[3] There is a significant investment in advertising for legal services. The amount spent seems to be increasing at a rapid rate. There are so many attorneys out there, and they want to make the public aware of their services. While advertisements can be found anywhere, from a billboard to a radio ad, the internet has introduced a new way for attorneys and law firms to advertise their services. And with the average individual in the US spending seven hours and three minutes on the internet every day, it is no wonder that firms seek to advertise their services online.[4]

I believe the amount of money spent on advertising and marketing in 2024 was significantly less than what will be spent during the next five years. The main reason is that, in addition to law firms and attorneys, we are beginning to see venture

---

2   American Tort Reform Association, *Legal Services in the United States: 2017–2021* (American Tort Reform Association, 2022), 5, https://www.atra.org/wp-content/uploads/2020/10/Legal-Services-Advertising-Report-United-States-%E2%80%93-ATRA-%E2%80%93-2017-2021-1.pdf.

3   "Legal Services Vertical—Insights into the US Local Ad Marketplace 2024," BIA Advisory Services, April 2024, https://shop.biakelsey.com/product/insights-into-local-advertising-legal-services-vertical.

4   Simon Kemp, "Digital 2024: Global Overview Report," DataReportal, January 31, 2024, https://datareportal.com/reports/digital-2024-global-overview-report.

capital firms entering the legal world and investing in law firms or lead generation companies. I will discuss this later.

LEGAL ADVERTISING AND THE INTERNET

In today's world, if we want information to assist us in making a wise and informed choice, we often go to the internet. If you are looking for a new restaurant to try out, you go online to look at menu options and to read reviews from other customers about portion sizes, atmosphere, and quality of service. If you want to purchase a new pair of running shoes, you go online to read reviews about style, support, and fit. This same thought process is frequently applied when it comes to choosing an attorney.

Many people look for information about their legal needs on the internet. In fact, 43 percent of those who sought legal assistance used Google searches to make their selection.[5] While many individuals find personal and professional referrals to be valuable and important, most people prefer to do their own research when it comes to finding an attorney that best fits their needs. Thus, to perform their own investigation, they look online to begin their search.

When those internet searches are made, about 62 percent are general and nonbranded.[6] For example, rather than searching the name of a specific law firm or attorney, the individual will

---

5   Martindale-Avvo, *Hiring an Attorney 2019: Legal Consumer Choices; Client Expectations* (Martindale-Avvo, 2019), 9, https://www.martindale-avvo.com/wp-content/uploads/Hiring-an-Attorney-2019.pdf.

6   Stephen Fairley, "Legal Marketing Stats Lawyers Need to Know," *The Rainmaker Blog, National Law Review*, October 1, 2015, https://natlawreview.com/article/legal-marketing-stats-lawyers-need-to-know#google_vignette.

often type their location and the type of attorney they are pursuing (e.g., "Indianapolis personal injury attorney"). Once they type their inquiry into the search bar, usually the search will produce a page of potential leads. At the top of the page will be attorney ads, sponsored attorneys, or law firms. Below the ads will be a listing of attorneys, law firms, or businesses that the search engine thinks are the most relevant for the inquiry. However, some of these online listings are not even attorneys or law firms. Instead, they are companies that harvest leads to sell to law firms they have a relationship with. The average law firm invests about 28 percent of its marketing budget into online marketing to make sure their information is available to the public.[7] Once the client has clicked on any of the listings, they will often be retargeted by that entity at a later time—even if the client didn't initially select that particular firm or attorney. Each of these attorneys or lead generation companies will likely have a form to fill out. These forms are simple and easy. The client fills out the form, then the law firm will communicate with them to see if they can assist the potential client. There is even software some companies use to call the client once they've put in their phone number—even before the user is done filling out the form. An individual can hire an attorney online without ever meeting or talking to an attorney.

But maybe you haven't even been specifically searching for an attorney—maybe you have just been going about your normal business online. Many people regularly enjoy and use social media like Facebook, Instagram, LinkedIn, YouTube, TikTok, and others. It is likely that if you use social media, you have

---

7   Alex Lindley, "61 Law Firm Marketing Statistics (2023)," *Law Firm Content Pros* (blog), December 10, 2022, https://lawfirmcontentpros.com/law-firm-marketing-statistics/.

encountered attorney ads. Social media is frequently used by firms to advertise their services. One survey found that 43 percent of law firms use ads on social media to advertise their services.[8] Certainly, if you have searched for any law firm, legal issue, or attorney, you will have received ads from the one you searched plus ads from others you didn't search for. Most of these ads will take you to the attorney's or a lead generation company's website. It will be easy to click a few boxes, fill out a short form, and easily and conveniently hire an attorney.

It has never been easier to find and hire an attorney. Attorney ads are everywhere. It is easy to make contact with these attorneys, and you can have one without even talking to an attorney. After all, you need only fill out a form, talk to an intake person, and sign the documents that they electronically send to you. It is easy and convenient.

The problem is that the attorney you choose might be the wrong attorney.

It has never been easier to find and hire an attorney, and it has never been easier to pick the wrong attorney.

---

8   "Marketing by the Numbers: Statistics on Legal Marketing in 2021 (and a Look at 2022)," *Justia: Legal Marketing & Technology Blog*, December 20, 2021, https://onward.justia.com/marketing-by-the-numbers-statistics-on-legal-marketing-in-2021-and-a-look-at-2022/.

CHAPTER 2

How Did We Get Here?

FIRST OF ALL, IT SHOULD BE NOTED THAT NOT EVERYONE
with a legal problem or issue hires an attorney. In fact, of
those that faced a legal problem between 2016 and 2018, only
65 percent hired a lawyer, and 22 percent of consumers avoid
hiring a lawyer, preferring to represent themselves or ignore the
problem when they face legal challenges.[9] The most common
areas where people are not obtaining professional help are wills
and estate planning, traffic tickets, driver's license issues, fami-
ly-related matters, debt, bankruptcy, personal injury, insurance
claims, and the sale or purchase of real estate.[10] However, if
you decide that you need legal assistance, how do you decide
which attorney to hire? How would you know which attorneys
would be able to help you with your specific need? Some people
may select an attorney or law firm based upon the advertisements that have been on billboards, television, or the internet.

---

9   Clio, *Legal Trends Report: 2018* (Clio, 2018), 24–25, https://www.clio.com/wp-content/uploads/2023/02/
    Legal-Trends-Report-2018.pdf.

10 Clio, *Legal Trends 2018*, 23.

However, such advertising has not always been available to the general public.

HISTORY OF LEGAL ADVERTISING

Before 1977, picking an attorney was pretty straightforward. There was no internet. There were no attorney billboards, phone book ads, bus or car wraps, direct mail from attorneys, TV ads, ads at sports events, or other types of highly visible attorney marketing. People tended to hire local attorneys from their city or the county seat. Most attorneys were located close to the courthouse or other county offices. The only advertising typically permitted was a business card and a sign outside of a law office.

In fact, prior to 1977, the American Bar Association (ABA) and the states that followed the ABA rules prohibited attorney advertising. A business card with the attorney and law firm's name, phone number, address, and the types of law practiced was permitted. Everything else was prohibited because it was claimed that advertising reflected negatively on the professionalism of the practice of law. Occasionally, you would see an ad in the local newspaper, which was simply a copy of the attorney's business card. However, that was the extent of advertising for attorneys.

Attorneys were involved in local service clubs, churches, politics, or other community groups. People tended to hire through a prior relationship or by word of mouth. Most law firms were general practice firms. This method of picking an attorney was advantageous for established law firms. The longer an attorney and the law firm practiced in the community, the more likely it was that people knew or had heard of that firm. As a result, many established law firms liked the status quo. They didn't need advertising and were against anything that could hurt their dominance.

In 1977, that all changed. In the United States Supreme Court, in a close decision (five to four), the majority ruled that an attorney's right to advertise was protected by the US Constitution.[11] The Supreme Court held that advertising would provide the public with valuable information about the availability and cost of legal services. They also held that attorney advertising wouldn't harm the profession or the administration of justice and would make such services more available to more people. The court also recognized how the ban on legal advertising was advantageous for established law firms and a hurdle for new attorneys with minimal contacts. Basically, the court put faith in the ability of the public to sort through attorney ads as they did other businessmen or professionals.

The ad that gave rise to this opinion was a small ad in a local Phoenix, Arizona, newspaper. Two attorneys, John Bates and Van O'Steen, decided they could charge a lower price for routine legal services if they could attract enough clients. They advertised "Legal Services at Very Reasonable Fees." They listed some of the services they provided and the cost of those services. The Arizona state bar filed an ethics complaint against the two attorneys. It was initially recommended that both attorneys be suspended for six months for the violation. The case then went up on appeal, eventually landing in the United States Supreme Court. By deciding that the attorneys' advertisement was pro-

---

11   Bates v. State Bar of Arizona, 433 US 350 (1977), Oyez, accessed July 8, 2024, https://www.oyez.org/cases/1976/76-316.

tected commercial speech, the Supreme Court forever changed the way attorneys marketed themselves and their services.

LEGAL ADVERTISING AND ETHICS

This decision to allow legal advertising opened the door to a whole new world of marketing for attorneys. Attorneys and law firms could now let people know how they could assist them, and people could more easily locate someone to assist with their legal needs. But now that attorneys could advertise their services, some further specifications were needed on what was allowed to protect the professionalism of the practice as well as the clients being served.

In 1978, *Ohralik v. Ohio State Bar Association* clarified the difference between advertising and solicitation. This case centered around an attorney, Ohralik, that heard about a car accident in his local community. Ohralik discovered the name of those injured by the accident, Carol McClintock and Wanda Lou Holbert, and sought to contact them at the hospital where they were receiving treatment. The attorney offered to provide services for each of the victims. Initially, both clients hired Ohralik. However, Holbert eventually decided she did not want to pursue legal action, and McClintock decided to hire another attorney. Furthermore, McClintock and Holbert filed an ethics complaint against Ohralik and his tactics to recruit them. This case made its way up to the Supreme Court, which helped to differentiate between the advertising of services and the solicitation of clients.[12]

---

12   Ohralik v. Ohio State Bar Assn., 436 U.S. 447 (1978), Oyez, accessed July 8, 2024, https://www.oyez.org/cases/1977/76-1650.

Ohralik's case led lawmakers to clarify that advertising serves as a way to communicate what services an attorney or law office can offer to consumers. Advertising simply lets people know where they can go to get the legal help that they need. On the other hand, solicitation is an advertisement of services that targets a specific group of clients or individuals.[13] This could be specifically targeting an individual who has experienced a crisis with an offer of legal assistance. This targeting could be directly calling the potential client or showing up at their home or place of employment to offer services. The nature of personal solicitation can tend toward intimidation, fraud, or undue influence. Thus, to protect those in need, such practices were prohibited.[14] Advertising can be monitored to make sure that it is accurate and truthful, while solicitation is harder to monitor as it is not open to public scrutiny.[15]

While every state bar has specific rules to be followed, there were certain standards to be upheld by attorneys and firms seeking to advertise their services. One such standard was that any advertising was to accurately represent the services that an attorney or their office could offer. If any part of the advertising is misleading or misrepresenting the truth, it is considered unethical.[16] This includes a misrepresentation of their experience, fees, and so on. Advertising permitted attorneys to let people know where they could find help for their legal needs.

---

13   Sharon Miki, "Lawyer Advertising Rules You Need to Know," *Clio* (blog), last updated February 13, 2025, https://www.clio.com/blog/lawyer-advertising-rules/.

14   Ohralik v. Ohio State Bar Assn.

15   Lauren Bowen, "Advertising and the Legal Profession," *Justice System Journal* 18, no. 1 (1995): 43–54, https://doi.org/10.1080/23277556.1995.10871221.

16   Model Rules of Prof'l Conduct R. 7.1 (Am. Bar Ass'n 2025), https://www.americanbar.org/groups/professional_responsibility/publications/model_rules_of_professional_conduct/rule_7_1_communication_concerning_a_lawyer_s_services/.

MODERNIZING THE STANDARDS

When the original laws and regulations around legal advertising first came to be, they were centered around the main methods of advertisement of the day. These media of advertisement included the Yellow Pages, newspapers, direct mail, radio, and television.[17] Today, however, the majority of advertisements from law firms are found online. According to one survey performed in 2021, law firms use a variety of online methods of advertising. When asked about common ways that law firms or attorneys advertise their services, they included the following: firm websites (78.2 percent), lawyer directories (58.2 percent), social media (43 percent), and Google Ads (23 percent).[18] Naturally, with the shift from newspaper and Yellow Pages ads to modern technology came a need to update ethical rules, options, and standards for legal advertising.

In 2018, the ABA House of Delegates changed and updated the Model Rules of Professional Conduct. The updates for these rules helped to clarify and modernize the rules for advertising.[19] One added update was that an attorney or law firm may advertise their services through any type of media. Not only could advertisements be placed on TV or radio, but advertisements were permitted on social media sites. Another clarification was that attorneys cannot imply that they are certified as a specialist unless they have officially been certified by a state, US territory,

17 Bowen, "Advertising and the Legal Profession," 53.

18 "Marketing by the Numbers: Statistics on Legal Marketing in 2021 (and a Look at 2022)," *Justia: Legal Marketing & Technology Blog*, December 20, 2021, https://onward.justia.com/marketing-by-the-numbers-statistics-on-legal-marketing-in-2021-and-a-look-at-2022/.

19 "Explained: Update to Advertising, Marketing Rules," American Bar Association, July 2019, https://www.americanbar.org/news/abanews/publications/youraba/2019/july-2019/explained--update-to-advertising--marketing-rules/.

or the ABA.[20] Additionally, an emphasis was made to further prevent solicitation of clients. These updates were set with the goal to uphold ethical standards for attorneys and law firms when it comes to advertising their services to clients—whether through TV ads, billboards, social media, or Google searches. Attorneys were permitted to advertise, but it was important that such advertisements were of an honest nature to protect clients.

USING THE INTERNET TO FIND AN ATTORNEY

Today, the majority of people seeking legal advice use an online search engine, such as Google.[21] One survey found that 57 percent of people use the internet when seeking to hire an attorney.[22] Potential clients may be investigating or searching for an attorney that they've heard of or been referred to. Even if a person receives a recommendation or referral for a certain attorney or law firm, many people prefer to hear about the experiences of others who have worked with the specific attorney or law firm. In a survey of sixty-three hundred people that have hired an attorney, 46.5 percent said online reviews from sources like Yelp, Avvo, and Google greatly impacted their decision when choosing an attorney.[23] People tend to trust the recommendations and reviews left by people online.

---

20 MODEL RULES OF PROF'L CONDUCT R. 7.2(C) (AM. BAR ASS'N 2025), https://www.americanbar.org/content/aba-cms-dotorg/en/groups/professional_responsibility/publications/model_rules_of_professional_conduct/rule_7_2_advertising/.

21 Stephen Fairley, "Legal Marketing Stats Lawyers Need to Know," *The Rainmaker Blog, National Law Review*, October 1, 2015, https://natlawreview.com/article/legal-marketing-stats-lawyers-need-to-know#google_vignette.

22 Clio, *Legal Trends Report: 2019* (Themis Solutions, 2019), 21, https://www.clio.com/resources/legal-trends/2019-report/.

23 Colleen Williams, "How Do Clients Research and Find Their Attorneys?," Martindale-Avvo, January 9, 2020, https://www.martindale-avvo.com/blog/how-do-clients-research-and-find-their-attorneys/.

Another recent survey found that 80 percent of people would check out an attorney's services online before hiring them. Sixty-four percent of people said that if they had a legal problem, they would start their research online. Twenty-one percent of those questioned said that they believed that Google ranked attorneys as "first" based upon the attorney's qualifications.[24] Other surveys have found similar results. It appears that the internet is the most popular way to not only research legal issues, questions, and problems, but also pick an attorney.

The internet has changed the way people find attorneys, which has changed the way law firms advertise their services. A person can easily access tons of information about legal issues, attorneys, or law firms by typing or speaking keywords or phrases into a search engine. People no longer must own or have access to a desktop computer to do their search. Many individuals use their smartphone or tablet to do their search. Anyone with access to a smartphone and Wi-Fi has all the information they need at their fingertips.

In today's world, searching for an attorney to represent you can be done in a matter of minutes. How, then, do law firms make their services known to potential clients? How do law firms grab the attention and notice of those seeking legal assistance? Like any other business, law firms utilize and invest in marketing.

---

24   Chris Rossi, "Legal Marketing Statistics Attorneys and Law Firms Need to Know in 2024," *Attorney Sluice* (blog), accessed July 8, 2024, https://attorneysluice.com/blog/legal-marketing-statistics-law-firms-need-to-know/.

THE INVESTMENT OF LEGAL MARKETING

Law firms spend a lot of money to get your attention. Certainly, the advertising and marketing efforts that most people see are primarily done by consumer practice law firms. The big spenders in consumer practice law firms are personal injury, criminal, bankruptcy, and divorce attorneys. That doesn't mean that law firms that handle corporate and business law don't engage in marketing. You often see these types of firms sponsoring professional sports teams, theaters, conventions, or business seminars. All types of law firms engage in marketing, and that marketing varies depending on the type of practice.

According to a recent study, the average law firm's marketing budget allocates 28 percent to online marketing, 19 percent to billboards and print ads, 17 percent to TV ads, 16 percent to networking, 14 percent to podcasts / radio spots, and 10 percent to other types of marketing.[25] It is often recommended that a law firm spend between 2 and 18 percent of its gross revenue on marketing.[26] Previously, the average amount spent was between 10 and 25 percent of the law firm's gross revenue. However, more recent stats indicate that the average amount spent is between 15 and 20 percent of the law firm's gross revenue.[27] Based on my experience, this amount seems rather low. Often, it seems that the more successful law firms spend more on their investments in legal marketing. However, the actual amount

25   Sohom Mukherjee and Chintan Zalani, "The Current State of Legal Marketing: Statistics 2025," On the Map Marketing, November 13, 2024, https://www.onthemap.com/law-firm-marketing/stats/.

26   Jason Hennessey, "How Much Should Law Firms Spend on Marketing?—2022 Guide," *National Law Review*, January 19, 2022, https://natlawreview.com/article/how-much-should-law-firms-spend-marketing-2022-guide.

27   Ivan Vislavskiy, "Important Law Firm Marketing Statistics," *Comrade Digital Marketing* (blog), January 30, 2025, https://comradeweb.com/blog/law-firm-marketing-statistics/.

spent depends on the size of the law firm, the market where the law firm is located, and the type of law the firm practices.

In 2021, $971.6 million was spent by law firms on TV ads alone. Firms also spent $253 million on outdoor ads and $99 million on radio ads.[28] A substantial amount of money is being spent to advertise available services to the public. A substantial amount of money is being invested to grab your attention. A substantial amount of money is being devoted to making it easy and convenient for you to hire an attorney.

However, with this plethora of available information and options accessible at our fingertips, there does seem to be a problem.

---

28 American Tort Reform Association, *Legal Services in the United States: 2017–2021* (American Tort Reform Association, 2022), 5, https://www.atra.org/wp-content/uploads/2020/10/Legal-Services-Advertising-Report-United-States-%E2%80%93-ATRA-%E2%80%93-2017-2021-1.pdf.

CHAPTER 3

The Problem

THE PROBLEM IS THAT IT IS EASIER IN TODAY'S MODERN world to pick the wrong attorney than to pick the right attorney. This is a huge problem. The average person has no idea how to pick the best attorney for their legal matter. They are bombarded with advertising and other marketing from attorneys who may not be the best fit for their issues. To make things even more confusing, one attorney may be the greatest at one type of case but inexperienced in another area. So she/he might be an excellent choice for the first situation and a bad choice for a different matter. Imagine for a moment that you find yourself in desperate need of an intricate and complicated heart surgery. However, when you go to hire a surgeon, you pick the best eye doctor in the state to do the surgery on your heart. I don't think so. Most people would probably agree that such a scenario would be rather foolish.

The difference between the surgeons in the scenario mentioned above and attorneys is that the eye surgeon isn't advertising for heart surgery cases. The eye surgeon isn't out seeking clients to hire him for their serious cardiac surgeries. However, unfortunately, many attorneys advertise outside of their expertise. When these unexperienced attorneys work with cases outside of their ability and experience, they either handle the case incompetently, learn on the job, or refer the case to someone you didn't choose. An example would be a divorce attorney that is just starting out and who has only handled very small and uncomplicated divorces. Is that the attorney you would want for a complicated divorce case involving large amounts of assets, pensions, retirement accounts, or custody issues? I wouldn't think so. Another example would be an attorney marketing for criminal cases, but who has only handled misdemeanors and simple cases. That probably isn't the attorney you want for a serious criminal matter that involves large fines or prison time.

An area of law that I am extremely familiar with is personal injuries or wrongful deaths that arise from a wreck with a semi–tractor trailer or other commercial motor vehicle. These are very complicated cases and are not the same as car crashes. The skillset needed to be successful with a large truck personal injury case isn't the same as the skillset needed to handle a slip and fall, medical malpractice, or car crash case. Yet I see attorneys advertising for truck wreck cases who have never handled these types of cases and who do not have the experience, knowledge, or resources needed to be successful.

Picking the wrong attorney can have devastating results for years, or even for your entire life. The wrong choice of an attorney can cause you and your family to not obtain the outcome you deserve. That is true regardless of whether it is an attorney handling a divorce case, a custody battle, a criminal case, corporate litigation, estate planning, a business matter, a personal injury, or a semi or large truck case. The higher the stakes, the more important it is to pick the best attorney, or attorneys, for that specific matter. You deserve to have the right attorney and team to protect your rights and fight hard for the outcome you deserve.

The fact that you are reading this book is a great first step. Next, you will want to implement the information provided in Chapter 5 and put in the effort to be sure that you have the right attorney for your case. The good news is that any good attorney will be happy to answer your questions and explain her/his qualifications before you hire them. Good attorneys won't pressure you or try to scare you into making an immediate decision without explaining why they are the right fit and qualified to help you. The right attorney will be happy to share their knowledge, experience, skill, and past results and to discuss similar situations they have handled in the past.

As I have mentioned, I have handled serious personal injury cases involving large trucks for over thirty-five years. My first truck case involved a fully loaded dump truck that went off a state highway through a parking lot, through a building, and ended up striking my client. The defense claimed a defective tire caused the wreck and harm to my client. It was a complicated case that was resolved favorably for my client on the first day of the jury trial. Since that time, I have handled serious personal injury and wrongful death cases involving semitractors, tractor trailers, wreckers, dump trucks, buses, farm trucks, grain semitrucks, garbage trucks, short buses, flatbeds, large pickup trucks, and delivery vans. These cases are far more complicated than a personal injury claim not involving a commercial motor vehicle. The cases involving a heavy truck wreck require knowledge of applicable federal laws, state laws, CDL (commercial driver's license) manuals, industry standards, heavy truck reconstruction, available electronics, heavy truck mechanical issues, telematics, and other industry-specific items.

Obviously, an accident between a car and a semi, or other big truck, is different than a criminal case, real estate matter, divorce case, custody battle, or as previously mentioned, even other accident cases. A law license allows an attorney to practice law. Any type of law. But that doesn't mean she/he is the right attorney for a particular case. As a practicing attorney with more than thirty-five years of experience, I have never met an attorney who I felt was capable of handling any and all types of legal matters. However, I do know attorneys who are extraordinarily good at specific areas of the law.

When choosing the best attorney for your legal matters, it is important that you choose someone who has the right type of expertise and experience. In the same way that you don't want to hire an eye surgeon to perform a lifesaving heart surgery, you don't want to hire an attorney with no experience to handle your legal matter. So how do you identify the attorneys that are not the best fit for you and your case?

CHAPTER 4

Picking the Wrong Attorney

IN THIS CHAPTER, I WILL EXPLORE HOW *not* TO PICK YOUR attorney. Picking an attorney by one of these methods may not mean that your legal matter is doomed—but it might. The more important the legal issue or case is, the more effort you should use to be sure that you select the right attorney. Picking an attorney from the following options is the wrong way and may have a devastating result on you and your family.

PERSONAL SOLICITATION

Some of you may remember the movie *The Verdict* with Paul Newman. Paul Newman played a Boston attorney, Frank Galvin, who was down on his luck and who had a drinking problem. In one scene, Frank Galvin was trying to drum up business. He looked through the obituaries to try to find possible wrongful death clients. Then he would visit the funerals of these people, even though he didn't know them or their families. In one scene, he approached a family member, said he knew the deceased, gave the family member his business card, and asked him to call to discuss a possible case. In the movie, the gentleman realized that Galvin didn't know his family and was lying to try and pick up business. The gentleman then ran Galvin out of the funeral home. This is a form of personal solicitation. Not all personal solicitations are this blatantly obvious, but they are just as blatantly unethical.

Never hire an attorney you do not know who personally solicits business on your case. Personally solicited business, either direct or indirect, is unethical and against the code of ethics all attorneys swear that they will follow. Despite this fact, there are attorneys who are willing to violate these rules, engage in unethical behavior, and lie to get a case. The bigger the case, the more likely you are to find this behavior. Although there are only a few attorneys who would do this, these few give all attorneys a bad name. Even worse, because the general public doesn't know that this outrageous behavior is considered unethical, people continue to hire these attorneys.

Attorneys are bound by the code of ethics. When an attorney passes the bar exam, they get sworn in and must promise that they will follow these rules. Every state has these rules, and the ABA prepares model rules that states can use in drafting their own rules. Every state upholds a rule that prohibits personal solicitations. The ABA Model Rule 7.3 provides:[29]

---

29   MODEL RULES OF PROF'L CONDUCT R. 7.3(a) (AM. BAR ASS'N 2025), https://www.americanbar. org/groups/professional_responsibility/publications/model_rules_of_professional_conduct/ rule_7_3_direct_contact_with_prospective_clients/.

(a) "Solicitation" or "solicit" denotes a communication initiated by or on behalf of a lawyer or law firm that is directed to a specific person the lawyer knows or reasonably should know needs legal services in a particular matter and that offers to provide, or reasonably can be understood as offering to provide, legal services for that matter.

Communication from an attorney is not considered to be solicitation if it is aimed at advertising to the general public. These appropriate forms of communication include media like billboards, internet advertisements, or TV commercials.[30] Paragraph (a) clarifies that solicitation is not just general advertisement, but a way for an attorney to specifically and intentionally pursue someone who needs legal representation or services. This is exactly what Paul Newman's character did. He directly advertised his services to people he knew were in need of assistance. The ABA prohibits such behavior.

The ABA Model Rule 7.3 also provides:[31]

(b) A lawyer shall not solicit professional employment by live person-to-person contact when a significant motive for the lawyer's doing so is the lawyer's or law firm's pecuniary gain, unless the contact is with a:

(1) lawyer;

---

30 "Rule 7.3 Solicitation of Clients—Comment," American Bar Association, April 17, 2019, https://www.americanbar.org/groups/professional_responsibility/publications/model_rules_of_professional_conduct/rule_7_3_direct_contact_with_prospective_clients/comment_on_rule_7_3/.

31 MODEL RULES OF PROF'L CONDUCT R. 7.3(b) (AM. BAR ASS'N 2025), https://www.americanbar.org/groups/professional_responsibility/publications/model_rules_of_professional_conduct/rule_7_3_direct_contact_with_prospective_clients/.

(2) person who has a family, close personal, or prior business or professional relationship with the lawyer or law firm; or

(3) person who routinely uses for business purposes the type of legal services offered by the lawyer.

Rule 7.3(b) is to prevent attorneys from advertising their services in "live person-to-person contact" when the motivating factor is the money that the attorney could make.[32] Any interactions that are aimed at persuading someone toward the attorney's services are not allowed if they are happening in real time. This means that meeting with someone in person, on a live telephone call, in a video meeting, or through other live forms of communication is disallowed. However, interactions like chat rooms, text messages, or emails are allowed since the potential client can easily cease communicating.[33] The ability for a client to easily get out of the conversation is what makes the difference. Clients should never feel cornered or stuck when seeking to find the best person to represent their case.

When a person needs legal services, they may find themselves feeling overwhelmed by the circumstances. Many times, when people need legal services, it is not under the happiest of conditions. Whether due to a divorce, car accident, or wrongful death, a client may be in an emotionally vulnerable position. This vulnerable position may prevent the client from being able to use reasonable judgment to make the best choice for themselves and their family. This decision can be especially difficult to make when in the presence of a pushy attorney insisting

---

32   MODEL RULES OF PROF'L CONDUCT R. 7.3(b).

33   American Bar Association, "Rule 7.3—Comment."

upon an immediate answer or response. The client may find themselves in a position where they are being intimidated, pressured, or manipulated into making a decision that they are not certain they want to make. Additionally, person-to-person contact puts other vulnerable individuals (those whose first language is not English, the elderly, or those who have cognitive disabilities) in a position where they are influenced to make a decision that may not be in their best interest. This rule helps to protect such vulnerable individuals from being targeted or taken advantage of by unethical attorneys.

The exceptions to this rule include if the potential client is another attorney, someone who has an existing relationship with the attorney, or someone who uses the attorney's services for their business. The reason for this exception is that it is not very likely that an attorney would overreach on someone who is a past client, somebody who is familiar with their rights, someone the attorney has a personal or professional relationship with, or a situation that is not of significant financial interest for the attorney.[34] However, paragraph (c) of ABA Model Rule 7.3 provides further protection for the client:[35]

> (c) A lawyer shall not solicit professional employment even when not otherwise prohibited by paragraph (b), if:

> (1) the target of the solicitation has made known to the lawyer a desire not to be solicited by the lawyer; or

---

34 American Bar Association, "Rule 7.3—Comment."

35 MODEL RULES OF PROF'L CONDUCT R. 7.3(c) (AM. BAR ASS'N 2025), https://www.americanbar.org/groups/professional_responsibility/publications/model_rules_of_professional_conduct/rule_7_3_direct_contact_with_prospective_clients/.

(2) the solicitation involves coercion, duress or harassment.

No one likes to be pestered—especially after you have clearly stated that you are not interested in the offer. Rule 7.3(c)(1) presents that, even if all the rules are being followed, an attorney cannot seek employment if the client has told the attorney that they do not want their services. If a client has communicated to the attorney that they aren't interested in being represented by that attorney, then the attorney should not continue to contact the person in need.

Rule (c)(2) clarifies that any form of intimidation, threat, or unwanted and persistent communication is barred. The conduct of attorneys is to be ethical at all times and should never involve threatening or manipulating people into receiving legal assistance. Every client deserves to be treated with respect and dignity. If this basic human right is being overlooked by the attorney, the individual seeking legal assistance is protected by this rule.

Paragraph (d) of ABA Model Rule 7.3 states:[36]

> (d) This Rule does not prohibit communications authorized by law or ordered by a court or other tribunal.

Paragraph (d) clarifies that if communications have been authorized by law, court, or tribunal, an attorney can reach out to potential clients. One example might be in notifying potential members that could be involved in a class action lawsuit. For

---

36 MODEL RULES OF PROF'L CONDUCT R. 7.3(d) (AM. BAR ASS'N 2025), https://www.americanbar. org/groups/professional_responsibility/publications/model_rules_of_professional_conduct/ rule_7_3_direct_contact_with_prospective_clients/.

example, imagine that a drug company produces a medicine intended to cure the common cold. Millions of people take this drug to get rid of the pesky sickness. However, the drug ends up causing a variety of serious illnesses for those that took the drug. While each of the millions of people could hire an attorney to represent them, a class action lawsuit brings all the people together to join in one lawsuit. All these millions of people, under one lawsuit, can compile resources, records, witnesses, and more in their efforts for justice. Thus, paragraph (d) would allow attorneys to reach out to people who took the drug to let them know that they are able to receive representation for the harm that has been done to them.

Paragraph (e) of ABA Model Rule 7.3 provides:[37]

> (e) Notwithstanding the prohibitions in this Rule, a lawyer may participate with a prepaid or group legal service plan operated by an organization not owned or directed by the lawyer that uses live person-to-person contact to enroll members or sell subscriptions for the plan from persons who are not known to need legal services in a particular matter covered by the plan.

A prepaid or group legal service plan provides affordable access to legal services. These plans can provide advice on, and representation in, legal matters (traffic violations, lease disputes, etc.) as well as things like preparing a will. These plans can provide access to a variety of different attorneys within a network and can help address legal matters before issues arise.

---

37   MODEL RULES OF PROF'L CONDUCT R. 7.3(e) (AM. BAR ASS'N 2025), https://www.americanbar.org/groups/professional_responsibility/publications/model_rules_of_professional_conduct/rule_7_3_direct_contact_with_prospective_clients/.

An attorney cannot start, manage, or run a prepaid/group legal service plan where she/he would have the ability to participate in live person-to-person solicitation of clients. The attorney cannot use such an arrangement to solicit clients to build their own caseload. An attorney can be involved in these groups if they are directing clients to other attorneys. But communication cannot be targeted at individuals for the attorney's own personal gain. However, the organization could be used to generally inform people of other attorneys that could offer legal services.[38]

So why are these types of interactions prohibited by the ABA? Well, the purpose of this rule is to protect clients and make sure that attorneys are behaving in an ethical manner. By enforcing this rule, the ABA is seeking to prevent clients from being harassed, taken advantage of, and manipulated by attorneys who only have their own financial gain in mind.

Even though every attorney knows it is unethical to personally solicit cases, it still happens. This is especially true when it comes to large and catastrophic injury or wrongful death cases. Because the potential fee for the attorney is so high, attorneys will risk their license to try and get these cases. I have seen this many times over the years. I had a case in Marion County, Indiana, where my client was in Methodist Hospital. The client had been in a wreck with a semi and had suffered several life-threatening injuries. While at the hospital, a man arrived and went into my client's room. This was before the client had made the decision to hire me. The man said he worked for a service that helped victims of accidents. He said

---

38   American Bar Association, "Rule 7.3—Comment."

the organization was a nonprofit and they just tried to make it easier for those wrongfully injured by others. He then gave my client a copy of the police report. He said he knew that the client would need the report, and he hoped that it would help. As he was leaving the room, he said, "Oh, by the way, just in case you decide to hire an attorney, I know a really good one," and he gave him an attorney's business card. My client didn't know this person or the attorney. This conduct is unethical.

The man visiting my client in the hospital is called a runner. A runner is someone who personally solicits clients for personal injury attorneys. They usually are not attorneys but are paid by an attorney for every client they sign up for the attorney. They sometimes use police scanners and go to the scene of an accident to solicit business. Runners will go to the hospital or to the homes of the injured person. Their goal is to sign a client for a particular attorney. However, this is inappropriate and is an attempt to circumvent the rule against personal solicitation. However, personal solicitation is unethical and improper even if the attorney uses someone else, other than themselves, to solicit the case. In some states, this conduct is not only unethical but illegal. In the state of Indiana, Rule 7.3(a) prohibits attorneys and their employees (or agents) from seeking clients in any form of real-time solicitation.[39] In this case, there is specific language to prohibit such unethical conduct by runners.

However, the runners will often lie about their purpose. I had another case in Missouri where the lady who became my client had a serious brain injury and was in a coma following

---

39 "Indiana Rules of Professional Conduct: Rule 7.1–7.5," State of Indiana, accessed July 8, 2024, https://cdn.ymaws.com/www.inbar.org/resource/resmgr/CLE_Speaker_Materials/IRPC_7.1-7.5.pdf.

a wreck with an eighteen-wheeler. While in the hospital, a runner watched for my client's husband. With social media, it isn't hard to figure out where people are and what people look like. He targeted my client's husband. The runner lied to my client's husband and told him that he was an air paramedic and that he had flown in the helicopter with his wife after the wreck. He said he held her hand and prayed for her, and just wanted to check in to see how she was doing. As he was leaving, he pulled out an attorney's business card and gave it to the husband. He told the husband that the attorney was great and that he should hire him for his wife's case.

Unfortunately, this improper conduct is seldom prosecuted by the state bar association or the prosecutor's office. Many times, no one knows about the conduct because the person who is targeted ends up hiring the unethical attorney without ever knowing that the conduct was improper and unprincipled. Since these unethical attorneys get away with it and it can be highly lucrative for their business, the conduct continues.

Hopefully, by being aware of this conduct, you will be on the lookout for unethical and potentially illegal activity. *Do not hire an attorney recommended by a runner.* If the attorney is unethical enough to breach the rules to contract you as a client, how do you know he/she isn't unethical enough to steal part of your settlement? Or to settle your case for far less than what it is worth just to make quick money?

I have also seen attorneys use doctor's offices or chiropractor's offices to use runners to get clients signed. They then refer the case to a particular attorney who is very much aware that the cases are coming in through a runner. Remember, an attorney cannot do something indirectly that she/he couldn't do directly. This is still considered to be unethical conduct. I have also heard about law firms paying wrecker drivers, and even police officers, to act as runners and to refer a case to an attorney for a fee. *All* these methods and tactics are unethical. Stay clear of these unethical attorneys.

DIRECT MAIL

Direct mail is not considered to be a form of personal solicitation because it comes through the mail and is not given to you in person. The rules are different for direct mail because you can just throw the mail away. It is not likely to influence you or play on your emotions and coerce you into signing a fee agreement like an in-person meeting might. Direct mail is effective because it targets specific individuals in need of certain legal representation. For example, attorneys use direct mail to acquire people who have committed a traffic violation, such as a DUI, for eminent domain proceedings, or victims of car accidents.

Each state has its own rules about direct mail. Although, generally, direct mail is allowed, there are guidelines that must be followed.

The ABA Model Rule 7.2 covers the guidelines for how an attorney may communicate their services. Attorneys may communicate their name, business address, email address, website, phone number, types of services offered, and other information to those who may need legal assistance. This can be beneficial for individuals who need an attorney to represent them for various matters.

However, there are certain ethical regulations that must be followed in relation to direct mail. For example, in the state of Indiana, a law firm or an attorney must wait a minimum of thirty days after an incident has occurred to send direct mail to solicit a client.[40] This mandatory waiting period is to protect the client who may have been harmed or grieving the loss of a loved one. This rule stands to protect clients who may be struggling emotionally, physically, or mentally.

The state of Indiana also requires that any written communication from an attorney, including direct mail, must include the words "advertising material" on the outside of the envelope and at the beginning of the communication. Whenever direct communication is sent, a copy must be filed with the Indiana Supreme Court Disciplinary Commission. Furthermore, the law office must keep a record of all such solicitations for a full year following the mailing date. This helps to make sure that attorneys are adhering to the requirements of the state in relation to direct mail solicitations.[41]

Additional advertising regulations also matter in relation to direct mail. If an attorney sends direct mail to a client, they must not imply that they are an expert in any field. The exception to this regulation is if the attorney has been officially certified as an expert by the ABA or the authority of the state. Additionally, if the attorney desires to list their areas of official

40   IND. R. PROF'L. COND. 7.3(b)(3) (IND. BAR ASS'N, November 4, 2024), https://casetext.com/rule/indiana-court-rules/indiana-rules-of-professional-conduct/information-about-legal-services/rule-73-contact-with-prospective-clients.

41   IND. R. PROF'L. COND. 7.3(c) (IND. BAR ASS'N, November 4, 2024), https://casetext.com/rule/indiana-court-rules/indiana-rules-of-professional-conduct/information-about-legal-services/rule-73-contact-with-prospective-clients.

expertise, they must list the name of the organization that has certified them as an expert.[42] Furthermore, attorneys should not make false or misleading statements about their services or abilities. For example, an attorney cannot guarantee success or promise a client a certain amount of money for their case. Another example would be a misleading statement about the firm's fees for services. Any information that is given must be accurate and truthful. Such misinformation can lead to disciplinary action.[43]

Regardless of the rules, and assuming that an attorney follows the rules and only sends direct mail how and when allowed, picking an attorney because of direct mail doesn't assure you that you are picking the right attorney. All it means is that the attorney is aggressive in marketing. Unfortunately, it doesn't mean they are the best qualified, experienced, knowledgeable, or the right fit for you.

TELEVISION ADVERTISEMENTS

Even though attorneys seem to be shifting some of their marketing budget away from television ads over to the internet, social media, and other forms of marketing, television is still one of the main vehicles used to attract clients. In an insurance journal article published in April of 2024, Rustin Silverstein, present of X Ante, stated that an estimated $1.2 billion was

---

42 MODEL RULES OF PROF'L CONDUCT R. 7.2(c) (AM. BAR ASS'N 2025), https://www.americanbar.org/content/aba-cms-dotorg/en/groups/professional_responsibility/publications/model_rules_of_professional_conduct/rule_7_2_advertising/.

43 "Comment on Rule 7.1," American Bar Association, accessed July 8, 2024, https://www.americanbar.org/groups/professional_responsibility/publications/model_rules_of_professional_conduct/rule_7_1_communication_concerning_a_lawyer_s_services/comment_on_rule_7_1/.

spent on TV ads by attorneys and others soliciting clients in need of legal services. He estimated that more than sixteen million ads for legal services ran on TV in 2023. That equals forty-five thousand ads every day, nineteen hundred every hour, and one ad every two seconds.[44]

Personal injury ads, such as car accidents, truck accidents, and other injury claims, account for most of the ads that are run. However, there has also been an increase in ads focusing on a specific topic. These ads can target injuries or deaths caused by prescription drugs, medical devices, baby powder, pesticide, or other dangerous consumer products, and storm damage claims. These specific mass tort ads are run not only by law firms/groups of law firms, but also by lead generation companies. According to Silverstein, in the past ten years, there have been around two thousand continually running mass tort ads.[45]

Certain markets are far more competitive than others, and it is impossible to turn on the television without seeing multiple attorney ads. Most legal ads on television will be ads for personal injury attorneys. Some of these commercials are very well done, professionally and informatively. They reflect well on the legal profession. Some are tacky, nonprofessional, and reflect negatively on attorneys. Of course, whether something is tasteful or not is in the eye of the beholder. What might make my skin cringe might not bother you at all. One attorney who advertises frequently on TV had two law firms. One law firm would advertise and use one name to sign up the clients.

---

44 Allen Laman, "Expert: 'Unceasing Onslaught' of Legal Ads Worth Your Attention," *Insurance Journal*, April 1, 2024, https://www.insurancejournal.com/magazines/mag-features/2024/04/01/766859.htm#.

45 Laman, "Unceasing Onslaught."

However, if the case didn't settle, he would transfer the case to his other firm with a different name so that when his attorneys went in front of a jury, their client wouldn't be adversely affected by the TV commercials. It is sad that a law firm has to worry that their ads are so distasteful that a jury might hold it against them in trial.

Attorney advertising on television has been, and continues to be, good for the public. People have been educated about their rights and the legal process. As advertising has increased, the attorneys seem to be doing more and more outrageous stuff to get your attention. For example, I have seen attorneys swinging large hammers, standing on top of semis, fighting aliens and robots, fighting dragons, and fighting zombies. Others I have seen rapping and singing. I have seen attorneys making it rain money and many other outrageous ads. Regardless, attorney television advertising has educated the public about such things as

- contingency fees—no fee unless the attorney gets the client money;
- not trusting insurance companies;
- the need to preserve evidence;
- the right to have an attorney;
- the rights of people accused of a crime;
- the rights of people going through a divorce; and
- the harm caused by dangerous products and medications.

But should you hire one of these attorneys who are advertising on television? The answer is *no*. At least not just because you saw their ad on television. The fact that an attorney is or is not on television is not a reason to pick that person to be your attorney. The fact that an attorney has decided to use television as part of their marketing strategy doesn't mean that they are skilled, knowledgeable, and a good fit for your legal matter. You should vet the attorney to be sure that she/he is qualified and is a good fit for you. This also doesn't mean that just because they are on television you shouldn't hire them. Simply, it just shouldn't be the deciding factor, or even a factor at all, in your selection process.

BILLBOARDS

If you live in a city with billboards, the odds are that they are used for attorney advertising. As long as the attorney follows the ethical rules for the state in which she/he practices, there is no problem against this form of advertising. I recently drove from Indianapolis, Indiana, to Atlanta, Georgia, and the majority of the billboards seemed to be for attorneys. Most of these were for personal injury attorneys.

Billboards are one of the most reasonably priced ways to market your law firm. These billboards are great for branding. The hope is, with daily driving by a billboard with the law firm's name on it, when you are faced with a need for representation, you will choose them. Personal injury attorneys are the most frequent users of billboards. However, you will also see attorneys advertising for workers' compensation, medical malpractice, divorces, criminal matters, employment, bankruptcy, and other consumer types of law. Just like television, there is no vetting going on in the selection of the attorneys who advertise via billboards. The billboard companies don't care if the attorney paying for the billboard is a good or bad attorney, an ethical attorney or an unethical attorney. All they care about is whether she/he can pay the monthly billboard fee.

Don't pick your attorney just because she/he is on a billboard. This doesn't mean that they are the best attorney to handle your case. I know some excellent attorneys who use billboards, but I also know some attorneys who aren't good who use them, and I certainly wouldn't hire them to represent me. The problem is that a nonattorney, or someone not involved in the legal arena, wouldn't know the good from the bad.

LEAD GENERATION COMPANIES

A lead generation company is a business that generates leads for attorneys. The number of lead generation companies and the amount of money that they are putting into the marketplace has grown dramatically within the past couple of years. Yet I believe we have only seen the tip of the iceberg. The amount of money coming from venture-capital-backed lead generation companies or law firms is about to explode. Some lead generation companies have no attorneys working for them. They are simply marketing companies. Others are law firms, but the attorneys are simply looking to acquire cases and then refer them out to other attorneys to collect the fees.

Some of these businesses simply provide law firms with the names and contact information of potential clients. Some companies provide law firms with signed clients. These companies are separate entities from the law firms. They work with multiple firms. Some lead generation companies sell the same lead to several law firms within the same market. Others sell the lead to just one law firm within a market.

These companies are not law firms. They are marketing companies that attract clients by online ads, television ads, radio ads, and through other companies. Their companies are particularly good at marketing campaigns. They obtain business, then sell the business to whichever law firm chooses to pay them. The problem is that these companies don't vet the law firm they sell the leads to. Instead, they sell to whoever wants, and can afford, to pay for the leads.

I recently did a Google search for the best truck wreck accident attorney in Indiana, and two of the top five listings were lead generation companies. They often have pay-per-click ads for top keywords. They also spend a lot of money on SEO. SEO stands for "search engine optimization," which is a marketing strategy to help a website to be viewed in various search engines like Google and Bing. What is concerning is that a person clicking on one of these ads will not be clicking on an attorney ad. Instead, they will be providing information to a company that will sell the information to a law firm.

This is not the way to pick an attorney. Don't turn the decision to make one of the most important decisions over to a marketing company that only cares about selling your case and making a profit. They may sell your case to a good law firm, or they may sell your case to a firm that is not the right law firm for your case. Be careful when researching a law firm to make certain that you are actually investigating a law firm. Some of the lead generation ads are deceiving and appear to be attorney ads rather than marketing campaign ads.

GOOGLE SEARCHES

According to Statista, 77 percent of consumers in the US, Germany, France, and the UK use Google when seeking information about local businesses.[46] Unsurprisingly, Google has become one of the most common ways people search for law firms. Although this is a great tool to find information about an attorney, law firms, or legal matters, it should be used properly. Just because someone appears at the top of the page does not mean that they are or aren't the best attorney for your legal matter. You should be aware of the following issues.

First, the top of the search page is usually full of ads—even though they may not look like ads. They list a law firm and look like the rest of the listings on the page except that they have the word "sponsored" at the top. A recent search for "a personal injury attorney to handle a severe truck wreck case in Indiana" had five sponsored listings before you ever got to the other Google list. These are simply paid ads. You do not have to qualify to get these top listings. Google doesn't vet these firms. These are simply attorneys who are paying for their location. They may be very skilled at what they are advertising, or they may be inexperienced and unqualified. Don't pick an attorney simply because they have a top "sponsored" listing. After you get past the sponsored listings, you will find the organic listings. Organic listings are unpaid listings that appear on the results page. The way Google designs the order of the organic searches is complicated and not fully understood. However, we do know a bit about how this process works.

In order for organic/unpaid listings to be placed toward the top of the page, Google considers a variety of factors. Each piece

---

46   Koen van Gelder, "Share of Consumers Using Search Platforms to Look for Local Business Information 2021," Statista, July 11, 2023, https://www.statista.com/statistics/1260363/consumers-using-search-engines-to-find-local-business-info/.

of content in a search needs to be linked to a variety of external and internal sources. For example, let's say you're reading a blog post from a doctor's office about best practices to stay hydrated in the summer months. In the post on hydration, there are links for previous blog posts from the doctor's office as well as articles from the Centers for Disease Control and Prevention and Mayo Clinic. From Google's perspective, this article becomes more relevant because it redirects the reader to further content on the individual site as well as links and connections to other well-known, reputable, and trustworthy websites. These connections and links are very important for Google to determine that content is useful. Another factor that is considered is if another website links their content to the site. So, in our example, a local news article refers its readers to the hydration blog post. This is considered a backlink structure, which elevates the relevance of the link from Google's perspective. Other important factors include how quickly the site loads, quality content and structure, videos and images, the ability for the website to be viewed on mobile screens, recognized keywords in the search, the amount of time typically spent on the page, and the quality of the encryption (safety and security) for the website.[47] In order for a website to be placed higher up on the search page, all these factors must be considered.

So if a law firm is listed at the top of the organic (nonsponsored) listings, then it is because Google determined, by utilizing complex ranking formulas, which law firm is relevant to your search inquiry. Certainly, by a higher ranking, this law firm has gotten Google's attention, and Google believes it is a good

---

47 Kinza Yasar, "Organic Search Results," TechTarget, last updated August 2022, https://www.techtarget.com/whatis/definition/organic-search-results.

fit. However, this doesn't mean that Google is right. In fact, Google isn't giving an opinion on whether a law firm is the right law firm for your legal matter. Don't pick a law firm just because they rank higher on the organic scale.

Another way Google organizes search results is by local maps. Typically, a local map will show three businesses that Google has determined should be listed based on your search inquiry. Google chooses these businesses by relevance (how much the business matches with the search), distance (how close the user is to the business), and prominence (how well known and liked the business is).[48] The prominence factor is based on Google reviews, ratings, backlinks, and how recognized the business is.[49] In 2021, Google began to consider distance as an incredibly significant factor. Because of this, businesses that are closer to the user will be recommended over others. So if you just type in "what is the best attorney to handle a speeding ticket," Google will recommend attorneys on the map that are close to you. However, this may not mean they are the best attorneys to represent you for your speeding ticket. First of all, the best attorney to handle your case may not be the closest to you. Wouldn't you prefer to drive across town to be sure you have the best attorney for your legal matter? The higher the stakes, the more likely you are to want the best attorney rather than simply having the closest attorney.

Use Google as a tool to help you find the best attorneys, but don't just pick a law firm because they are first on the list. Do

---

48 Arthur Andreyev, "Google Maps SEO: The Ultimate 2025 Guide to Boost Your Local Visibility," *SEO PowerSuite* (blog), February 19, 2025, https://www.link-assistant.com/news/google-maps-ranking.html?utm_source=linkedin&utm_medium=blog&utm_campaign=sps-social.

49 Andreyev, "Google Maps SEO."

your due diligence to be sure that the law firm is one with the experience, knowledge, skill, and resources to protect your rights and fight for you.

TARGETED ADS

When you are on the internet, regardless of whether it's You-Tube, LinkedIn, Facebook, Instagram, or other sites, you undoubtedly see targeted ads. Often these ads appear to show up out of nowhere, yet they are for businesses that are selling something we are interested in. Have you ever been talking with your friends or family about a food you have been craving? Or a gadget that you have been considering? Maybe you are talking about spaghetti or a new smartwatch, and you open your phone to see an advertisement for an Italian restaurant or a deal on smartwatches on Amazon. It is almost like our cell phones or computers listen to our conversations and then generate an ad for something we are thinking about. The truth is that, when these situations arise, we are seeing targeted ads. Marketers are very sophisticated and, therefore, exceptionally good at getting ads in front of people who are potential customers or clients. One way that marketers can target us is through something called geofencing.

Geofencing is a digital or virtual perimeter around a real geographic region.[50] These perimeters can encompass a distance within a certain area or be related to locations (like restaurants and stores). Due to location-based technology, various businesses can track where we are and direct ads to lure us to

---

50 Justin Croxton, "What Is Geofencing and How Does It Work? Location Based Software," Propellant Media, November 2, 2023, https://propellant.media/what-is-geofencing/.

purchase their products. This location-based technology can be through our Wi-Fi, cellular data, GPS software, and more. So, for example, say that you are walking through the mall. If you have an app on your phone for an ice cream shop and you pass within a certain distance, geofencing technology might lead to an advertisement or coupon for that ice cream shop. For example, "Today only: buy one, get one free on all single scoops!"

So how might geofencing be used in attracting clients to a law firm?

A criminal defense attorney could geofence a jail where someone is arrested and is concerned that they may be held unlawfully. Assuming that the person is given their cell phone back when they are getting relocated, then they could be geofenced and begin seeing ads for criminal defense attorneys. The same could be true for a hospital. A personal injury attorney could geofence a hospital or therapy facility so that the injured person, or their family who visits them, starts picking up ads for the law firm. If the ads don't violate any of the advertising ethics rules, these ads are probably ethical. This doesn't mean the particular law firm is the right choice. I have never engaged in geofencing hospitals and the like but have heard of other firms who do. They say it is no different than having a billboard across the street from the hospital. I am not here, nor is the purpose of this book, to weigh in on what is proper or improper advertising. Just because I am not comfortable doing something doesn't make it wrong. But like all advertising, just because someone gets an ad in front of you doesn't mean this is the attorney you should pick. Just because they are skilled at targeting marketing advertisements doesn't mean they are skilled at solving the legal issues you're facing. You are not looking for the best marketer. You are looking for the *best* attorney.

RETARGETING

Retargeting allows a business to reach back out to us after we have used their app or visited their website. So let's imagine you are looking to purchase a new recliner chair. You visit a website but decide that you aren't quite ready or sure that you want to buy that recliner. You close out of the website and move on with your day. Retargeting allows paid ads from the recliner website to "follow" you around in the hope that you will eventually return to the site and purchase their recliner. As you check Facebook to see what your friends are up to, lo and behold, an advertisement for the recliner is in the corner. The goal is that, sooner or later, you won't be able to stop thinking about the recliner and will just go ahead and order it.[51]

When it comes to searching for a law firm, you may have looked around on the site of a particular attorney but decided to wait before reaching out to them. Or maybe you even decided that law firm or attorney wasn't the best fit for you. With retargeting, the ad for that particular attorney or law firm can "follow" you around as you visit various sites. As with anything else, the hope is that you will see their name and consider having them represent you in your legal matter.

---

51 Michal Wlosik, "What Is Ad Retargeting and How Does It Work?," Clearcode, May 15, 2024, https://clearcode.cc/blog/what-is-ad-retargeting/.

GOOGLE ADS

Google Ads is an online advertising program used by Google to connect people with products and services.[52] Google Ads is based on a pay-per-click format where a company pays for each click they receive on an advertisement. The hope with these paid ads is to direct customers to businesses that meet their needs. These ads are focused on the keywords that individuals type in when searching for their desired product. When companies choose to use Google Ads, a list of keywords is compiled to connect the customer with the company's product(s).[53] Unlike organic search results, a business has to pay for their ads to appear on the Google search results.[54]

Be careful that when you Google an attorney or law firm's name, you actually click on whom you are looking for. So let's say that you are following my advice on how to select an attorney. You want to research the attorney. You start with a Google search—you type in the name of the attorney. What you might not realize is that some law firms bid on the names of their competitors. So their "sponsored" ad appears on the top of the attorney's page that you are searching for. Unfortunately, I have seen ads where the attorney hides their true identity. On the ad, they will put a phone number in bold and a general message to call to get a consultation. If someone is looking for law firm "X," they may end up calling law firm "Y"

52 "Google Ads: Definition," Support, Google, accessed July 8, 2024, https://support.google.com/google-ads/answer/6319?hl=en.

53 "Google Ads: What Are Google Ads & How Do They Work?" WordStream, accessed July 8, 2024, https://www.wordstream.com/google-ads.

54 Tiffani Anderson, "Overview of Google Ads (Formerly Adwords) and How to Use It," Bluehost, April 7, 2023, https://www.bluehost.com/blog/google-ads/.

without realizing it. Like I said, it has never been easier to end up with the wrong attorney.

OTHER LEGAL ADVERTISING

If you listen to the radio in large markets, an attorney is likely sponsoring the station and has their name showing up on your digital screen in your vehicle. If you go to professional or college sports events, they typically have law firms sponsor the event. Even some high school teams are sponsored by law firms. Local community safety events or other community events are often sponsored by law firms.

First of all, I think that it is great that law firms are active in their communities and sponsor various local teams and events. I especially think it is very positive that law firms are big supporters of small community projects. Attorneys regularly do good things for good reasons. However, the fact that a law firm is a sponsor of these events may not mean they are the best law firm for your type of case. Certainly, it may be a good place to start your search. Supporting law firms that are supporting the community is a good thing. However, you still want to do your due diligence.

Car wraps and bus wraps are also becoming more prevalent. There are even companies that can sponsor a concert or support large events. For supporting these events, the companies will surround the event with the law firm's logo all over the wrapped vehicle. This is excellent for branding. Just like all other forms of advertising, the fact that you see an attorney or law firm everywhere doesn't mean they are good or bad for your case or legal matters. It simply means they have a large marketing budget.

The bottom line is that a good marketer doesn't equal a good attorney. No matter what type of marketing is being used, you must not base your decision on the ad or marketing efforts. In addition, do not assume that all legal marketing is being done by an attorney or law firm. Lastly, don't be tricked when clicking on a law firm pretending to be someone else. The more important the legal issue you face, the more important it is not to pick the wrong attorney just because of advertising or marketing.

Just because you have heard a law firm's name advertised on TV, a Google Ad, or a billboard does not mean that they will be the best fit. There is so much to consider when selecting an attorney who is experienced and qualified enough to handle your case. How do you hire the right attorney for you and your case? In the following chapter, I will teach you how to do just that.

CHAPTER 5

Picking the Right Attorney

YOU NEED AN ATTORNEY. CLEARLY, YOU WANT TO HIRE
the right attorney for your legal matter. This chapter will focus
on steps you can take to help make sure the attorney you
choose has the experience, skill, knowledge, and resources to
handle your problem or legal need. Picking the wrong attorney
can have devastating results. Picking the right attorney can
make a huge difference for you and your family.

As you have seen from previous chapters, attorneys are des-
perately trying to get their name and their law firm's name in
front of you to get you to choose them. Some of these may
be good choices, and some of these are bad choices. Don't
just pick someone because you have seen their name. Instead,
choose wisely—your future may depend on it. Here are some
suggestions and helpful factors that you should consider as you
are seeking to pick the right attorney.

REFERRAL FROM SOMEONE YOU TRUST

A good place to start is a referral from someone that you trust. It could be that a family member or business colleague may have been through a similar legal situation. However, be sure that the experience is with the same type of legal matter. Just because a family member or friend had a successful result with an attorney handling a speeding ticket, this doesn't necessarily mean that the same attorney would be the right choice for handling a more serious criminal matter.

Likewise, someone who can handle a simple car crash injury case may not be the right person to handle a wrongful death, medical malpractice, procedural liability, or semi–car accident case. A divorce attorney may not be the best to give business advice. So if you get a referral from someone, ask follow-up questions about the specifics of their case. It is important to be sure that their case is similar to or the same as the matter you have.

If the recommended attorney has handled the same type of case or legal matter, then this is a good place to start. A happy client, someone with personal experience, is a great way to find the right attorney.

BOARD CERTIFICATION

One of the best ways to pick an attorney is to find one that is board certified. The American Bar Association (ABA) was founded in 1878 and is currently the largest voluntary association of attorneys and legal professionals in the world. One of the goals of the ABA is to improve the profession through legal education and by promoting competence, ethical conduct, and professionalism. One of the ways the ABA mandates competency of attorneys is by recognizing some attorneys who demonstrate expertise in a particular area of law through board certification.

The purpose of board certification is to recognize attorneys who have met higher standards of education, knowledge, and experience in specific areas of the law. The ABA presently accredits eighteen specialty certification programs. They recognize eight different private organizations that demonstrate the standards necessary to be board certified and to determine if an attorney qualifies for the board certification.

The eight private organizations and eighteen specialty programs that the ABA approved to determine board certification are:[55]

1. THE AMERICAN BOARD OF CERTIFICATION

This nonprofit organization certifies attorneys in the areas of business bankruptcy, consumer bankruptcy, and creditors' rights law. The American Board of Certification (ABC) has qualified almost one thousand attorneys in the areas of consumer, business bankruptcy, and creditors' rights law.[56] When it comes to consumer bankruptcy laws, the ABC provides certification for attorneys who represent debtors, creditors, and trustees. This area of involvement really focuses on Chapters 7 and 13. In relation to business bankruptcy law, the ABC

---

55 "Private Organizations with ABA Accredited Lawyer Certification Programs," American Bar Association, accessed July 8, 2024, https://www.americanbar.org/groups/specialization/organizations-with-aba-accredited-lawyer-certification-programs/.

56 "About ABC Board Certification," American Board of Certification, accessed July 8, 2024, https://www.abcworld.org/.

certifies practicing attorneys who help clients eliminate or restructure their debts when they are unable to pay. As for creditors' rights, the ABC certifies attorneys who help creditors who are seeking to claim money owed by debtors.[57]

2. THE AMERICAN BOARD OF PROFESSIONAL LIABILITY ATTORNEYS

The American Board of Professional Liability Attorneys (ABPLA) focuses on making sure attorneys are qualified and competent when it comes to handling cases of legal and medical malpractice. They thoroughly vet attorneys in this particular field to ensure that potential clients will be taken care of. To become board certified by ABPLA, malpractice attorneys are assessed in relation to experience, ethics, education, examination, and excellence. To be ABPLA certified, attorneys must adhere to the following basic requirements: pass a written examination, complete a minimum of thirty-six continuing legal education hours in the specified field, and provide ten references (five judges and five attorneys in the specified field). Depending on whether the attorney is being certified in medical or legal malpractice, further action is required. Some of these requirements include a minimum amount of time in the field, certain percentages of time spent focusing on such practice, and so on.[58]

You may need a medical malpractice attorney if you suffered harm from a delayed diagnosis or misdiagnosis. Other exam-

---

57 "Certification Areas," American Board of Certification, accessed July 8, 2024, https://www.abcworld.org/certification-areas.

58 "About ABPLA," American Board of Professional Liability Attorneys, accessed July 8, 2024, https://www.abpla.org/general-information.

ples could include harm from surgical or anesthesia errors, or improper medical care that led to harm. You may consider hiring an attorney for legal malpractice if an attorney missed deadlines that led to significant financial loss, when an attorney misuses finances in relation to your case, or a lack of consent, and more.

3. INTERNATIONAL ASSOCIATION FOR PRIVACY PROFESSIONALS

The International Association of Privacy Professionals (IAPP) is a nonprofit that strives to help attorneys who are experts in managing risk and protecting data.[59] The IAPP offers four potential certifications in the area of risk management and data protection.

The first is in AI (artificial intelligence) Governance. This certification is for attorneys who understand how AI works and how to responsibly navigate these sophisticated systems. This certification also relates to laws in relation to AI, navigating concerns related to AI, and making sure the public is safe in relation to AI systems.[60]

The second is the Certified Information Privacy Professional. This category focuses on attorneys who can demonstrate competence when it comes to data privacy laws and regulations.[61]

---

59 "About," International Association of Privacy Professionals, accessed July 8, 2024, https://iapp.org/.

60 "IAPP Certification," International Association of Privacy Professionals, accessed July 8, 2024, https://iapp.org/certify/aigp/.

61 "CIPP Certification," International Association of Privacy Professionals, accessed July 8, 2024, https://iapp.org/certify/cipp/.

The third is the Certified Information Privacy Manager. This certification relates to day-to-day interactions when it comes to data privacy laws.

The fourth in this category is Certified Information Privacy Technologist. This focuses on safety and protection practices for the products and services that we use every single day. Attorneys with this certification understand the laws relating to how our data can be monitored, saved, and used. This certification helps to make sure that companies and business are respecting our rights as citizens.[62]

4. NATIONAL ASSOCIATION OF COUNSEL FOR CHILDREN

The National Association of Counsel for Children (NACC) prepares and trains attorneys who represent children, families, and the related agencies. They provide certification for attorneys who are experienced in and informed about the area of child welfare law.[63] This certification is only granted to attorneys who go through an intense application and assessment process. To apply for certification, an attorney must have been practicing law for at least three years; have dedicated 30 percent of their time (within the last three years) to the field of child welfare law; have a résumé listing involvement in the field; obtain thirty-six hours (within the last three years) of continuing legal education in the area of child welfare law; and provide a writing sample demonstrating analysis of the

---

62   "CIPT Certification," International Association of Privacy Professionals, accessed July 8, 2024, https://iapp.org/certify/cipt/.

63   "Our Work," National Association of Counsel for Children, accessed July 8, 2024, https://naccchildlaw.org/.

field, public and private disciplinary history, and peer review responses. Someone may need an experienced child welfare attorney when it comes to matters like adoption, foster care, and guardianship when the state is involved.[64]

5. NATIONAL ASSOCIATION OF ESTATE PLANNERS & COUNCILS

The National Association of Estate Planners & Councils (NAEPC) strives to regulate excellence for attorneys who work in estate planning. The NAEPC recognizes that attorneys will be working with people at all stages of life and desire to protect these clients and their wealth and legacy.[65] To be certified, attorneys must be licensed to practice law, have twelve hours of continuing legal education in estate planning (within thirty-six months), pass an exam, have five recommendations from practicing peers, and have professional liability insurance coverage.

Estate planning attorneys with this certification specialize in putting together last wills and testaments, living wills, and trust funds and naming a financial/medical power of attorney. Certified estate planning attorneys may be especially helpful for estate planning and wills if you have a large family, have children who are minors, have family members with special needs, own a family business, and more.

---

64 "Child Welfare Law Specialist Certification," National Association of Counsel for Children, accessed July 8, 2024, https://naccchildlaw.org/cwls-certification/.

65 "Mission Statement / Vision Statement," National Association of Estate Planners & Councils, accessed July 8, 2024, https://www.naepc.org/about/mission.

6. NATIONAL BOARD OF TRIAL ADVOCACY

The National Board of Trial Advocacy (NBTA) is a nonprofit organization that oversees and certifies eight specialty areas. These include the following: civil trial law, civil practice advocacy, complex litigation, criminal trial law, family trial law, patent litigation, Social Security disability law, and truck accident law. The NBTA endeavors to help clients find an experienced legal representative for trial advocacy.[66]

Civil trial law focuses on noncriminal cases in areas like personal injury, real estate, or estate planning. These attorneys can help their client(s) as they are filing a lawsuit, working through court proceedings, and more. For an attorney to become certified in civil trial law, they must have five years of experience practicing law, spend at least 30 percent of their time practicing civil trial law within three years (includes participating in forty-five days of trial time, participating in at least one hundred hours of contested matters, etc.), participate in forty-five hours of continuing legal education in the area, submit ten to twelve peer references, pass an examination, and submit a copy of a legal writing document.[67] This certification is largely focused on trial skills.

Civil practice advocacy is practicing law between two parties. In order for an attorney to receive certification in this area, they must be in good standing, have been involved in at least one hundred contested matters, have forty-five hours of continuing legal education in the area, submit ten peer references, pass an

---

66 "About Us," National Board of Trial Advocacy, accessed July 8, 2024, https://www.nbtalawyers.org/about/.

67 "National Board of Trial Advocacy Standards for Civil and Criminal Certification: Civil Trial Advocates," National Board of Trial Advocacy, last revised May 2024, https://www.nbtalawyers.org/wp-content/uploads/2021/09/STANDARDS-CIV-TRIAL-CERT-CLEAN-COPY-7-8-21.pdf.

examination, submit a legal writing document, and submit a disclosure of conduct.[68] This certification is focused on the civil litigation process but is not as trial focused as the civil trial law certification.

Complex litigation involves court cases that involve a variety of complicated factors. These could be multiple parties and their attorneys, complicated subject matter, complex laws, substantial amounts of money, and more. Certification for complex litigation includes being in good standing, having practiced for ten years (and practicing in complex litigation for five), dedicating 35 percent of their time to complex litigation cases, involvement in one hundred contested legal matters, participation in forty-five hours of education in complex litigation, submitting ten peer references, passing a written examination, submitting a copy of a legal writing document, and a submitting a disclosure of conduct.[69] Some examples of complex litigation could include class action lawsuits (like a drug company that is sued because their product caused serious illness), intellectual property suits, environmental law, and more.

Criminal trial law deals with felonies and misdemeanors as they go to state and federal trials, as well as appellate courts. Qualifications for this certification include good standing in the practice, practicing for five years, 30 percent of time involved with criminal trial law, participation in seventy-five contested

---

68   "National Board of Civil Pretrial Practice Advocacy (NBCPPA)," National Board of Trial Advocacy, last revised May 2024, https://www.nbtalawyers.org/wp-content/uploads/2019/09/1-STANDARDS-CIV-PRACT-CERT-REVISED-4-27-18.pdf.

69   "Certification Standards: Complex Litigation Advocates," National Board of Trial Advocacy, last revised May 2024, https://www.nbtalawyers.org/wp-content/uploads/2021/03/STANDARDS-COMPLEX-LITIGATION.pdf.

matters, forty-five hours of continuing legal education in the subject, submitting ten to twelve peer-reviewed references, passing an examination, submitting three legal writing documents, and submitting a disclosure of conduct.[70] Attorneys certified in criminal trial law may deal with cases involving rape, assault and battery, drug charges, robbery, voluntary manslaughter, child pornography, stalking, and more.

Family trial law involves settling a dispute in a court of law when it involves familial relationships like husbands and wives, parents and children, and so on. Attorneys seeking to receive certification must be in good standing, have practiced law for five years, have dedicated 30 percent of their time to family trial law, have participated in forty-five hours of continuing legal education, submit ten to twelve peer references, pass an examination, submit a legal writing document, and submit a disclosure of conduct.[71] Attorneys certified in family trial law can assist with divorce, child custody and visitation arrangements, child support, domestic abuse, and more.

Patent litigation involves a dispute regarding the owner of a patent and their effort to sue someone else for creating, distributing, profiting from, or using the invention without the owner's consent. Certification in this area requires good standing in the law practice, active practice for at least five years, 35 percent of time devoted to patent litigation, one hundred

---

70 "National Board of Trial Advocacy Standards for Civil and Criminal Certification: Criminal Trial Advocates," National Board of Trial Advocacy, last revised May 2024, https://www.nbtalawyers.org/wp-content/uploads/2021/12/1-STANDARDS-CRIM-TRIAL-CERT.pdf.

71 "National Board of Trial Advocacy Standards for Civil and Criminal Certification: Family Trial Law Advocates," National Board of Trial Advocacy, last revised May 2024, https://www.nbtalawyers.org/wp-content/uploads/2019/09/1-STANDARDS-FAM-CERT.pdf.

hours of contested matters, thirty-five hours of continuing legal education, ten peer references, passing an examination, submitting a legal writing document, and submitting a disclosure of conduct.

Social Security disability law helps to represent individuals for disability and retirement benefits. Certification requirements include the following: being a lawyer in good standing, having practiced law for five years, 30 percent of time dedicated to the area, thirty-six hours of continuing legal education in Social Security disability law, ten to twelve peer references, an examination, six legal writing samples, and a disclosure of misconduct. Those certified in this type of law can greatly assist clients as they seek to make a case for receiving disability.

Truck accident law involves working with those who have been involved in accidents with tractor trailers, buses, semis, and other commercial motor vehicles. Certification for this area of expertise includes being in good standing in the state, having spent five years in the practice of truck accident law, devoting 30 percent of time to truck accident law, having forty-five hours of continuing education related to the area, twelve peer references, passing an examination, submission of a legal writing document, and disclosure of conduct.[72] Those qualified to assist with this type of law can help to make sure that you get what you deserve when you have been injured in such an accident.

---

72 "Certification for Truck Accident Advocates," National Board of Trial Advocacy, last revised May 2024, https://www.nbtalawyers.org/wp-content/uploads/2019/09/1-Standards-for-Truck-AccidentMAIN.pdf.

7. NATIONAL COLLEGE FOR DUI DEFENSE, INC.

The National College for DUI Defense (NCDD) certifies attorneys that are the most experienced and educated in the area of DUI cases. When it comes to DUI (driving under the influence) cases, the NCDD helps clients identify the right attorney that understands the laws regarding DUIs in their state and the legal issues and related circumstances that can impact these cases.[73] To become certified in DUI defense law, an attorney must practice DUI defense law for at least five years, devote a minimum of 50 percent of time to the area, have been a lead defense counsel in a minimum of fifteen DUI trials to verdict/judgment, have completed thirty-six educational hours in the area, and be eligible to practice law in the US.[74] You may consider hiring a certified attorney for a DUI if you were caught driving under the influence of drugs or alcohol.

8. NATIONAL ELDER LAW FOUNDATION

The National Elder Law Foundation (NELF) is an organization that certifies attorneys in the area of elder and special needs law. The NELF provides consumers with a list of attorneys that can provide expertise, skill, and care when working with cases involving seniors, families, and individuals with special needs.[75] Elder law attorneys work with elderly clients or their families in relation to legal matters like Medicaid planning to protect financial assets, nursing home placement and/or environment

---

73 "Mission Statement," National College for DUI Defense, accessed July 8, 2024, https://www.ncdd.com/about-the-ncdd/mission-statement.

74 "How to Become Board Certified in DUI Defense Law," National College for DUI Defense, accessed July 8, 2024, https://www.ncdd.com/board-certification/how-to-become-board-certified-in-dui-defense-law.

75 "Setting the Standard in Elder Law," National Elder Law Foundation, accessed July 8, 2024, https://www.nelf.org/.

management, elder abuse, preparing estate documents, and establishing trust funds. To be certified by NELF, an attorney must be licensed to practice law, practice for at least five years, be in good standing with the bars in which they are licensed, spend an average of sixteen hours per week practicing elder law, have handled a minimum of sixty elder law matters within three years, have forty-five hours of continuing legal education in the area, submit five professional peer references from attorneys in the area, and pass an examination.[76]

9. BOARD-CERTIFIED ATTORNEYS

A board-certified attorney, by any of the aforementioned groups, has demonstrated that she/he has significant experience, knowledge, and expertise in a specific area of the law. Not all attorneys are trained equally or have the same level of knowledge or experience. By picking a board-certified attorney, you are picking a true specialist. Each of the certified organizations sets the strongest standards of ethics, experience, and knowledge of the specific areas of law. The attorneys who are board certified concentrate a large part of their practice on a specific area of the law, they pass an examination on that area of law, they have experience in that area, and they are involved in continuing education in that area. Plus, they must renew the certification periodically. This helps ensure that the attorney you are investigating is still on top of their area of the law.

By picking a board-certified attorney, you are picking an attorney who has been vetted by a professional organization

---

76 "Preparing for the Exam," National Elder Law Foundation, accessed July 8, 2024, https://nelf.memberclicks. net/qualifications.

that understands what is necessary to set that attorney apart from and above other attorneys in that area of specialty. All attorneys have to be licensed but do not need to be board certified. Being board certified in a specialty shows that an attorney has gone above and beyond by having a higher level of expertise.

There are multiple benefits to having a board-certified attorney, such as

1. attorneys are vetted by professionals that know what makes an attorney a specialist in their area of practice;
2. expertise and knowledge of a specific area that is above that of most attorneys;
3. ability to handle more complex matters;
4. ongoing education in that area; and
5. peer review (attorneys and judges are involved to confirm expertise).

But how do you find a board-certified attorney?

It is incredibly easy to locate board-certified attorneys in your area. On all of the websites of the eight certification organizations, there is a way to locate a certified attorney in your area or state. When you are going to the websites of these organizations, you can trust that the listed attorneys have been certified and are qualified and experienced enough to handle your case or legal matter. For many of the organizations, the home page lists an option to "Find a Certified Attorney" or "Search Accredited Attorneys." Fortunately, with these websites, it is easy to find a board-certified attorney.

So if your legal issue, case, or matter falls within one of the categories where there is an ABA-approved board certification, then that would be a great place for you to start. This doesn't mean that all attorneys who are not board certified couldn't qualify. There are attorneys who could meet the standards to be board certified but have chosen not to take the time to go through the process. However, you don't know who they are. Picking someone who is board certified assures that you are picking someone who has more experience and knowledge than most other attorneys in a particular area of the law. To be board certified, you can't buy your way into the group. You must qualify.

SPEAKERS AND WRITERS

Additional ways you can tell if someone has more knowledge or skill is if they have written books, chapters in books, articles, or blogs in the area of law you are looking to hire. Research the attorney you are thinking about. Look to see what scholarly writings he/she has written on the subject that has given rise to your need for an attorney. Also look at what conferences they have spoken at and what subjects they have spoken about and how these apply to your needs. Additionally, listen to a podcast that they have been a guest on or, better yet, any podcast they might host. Again, be sure the subject matter discussed has something to do with your needs. A podcast that an attorney hosts about who serves the best hot dogs might be entertaining, but it tells us nothing about that attorney's knowledge, experience, or expertise. However, it would be a podcast I would love to host.

PEER-REVIEWED RANKING ORGANIZATIONS

There are organizations that rank or provide peer reviews of attorneys. Peer review simply means that other attorneys and/or judges are asked about the attorney through reviews. For example, one of the oldest ranking services is Martindale–Hubbell. Below are some of the websites that I consider to be helpful in considering whether or not to select an attorney:

1. **Martindale–Hubbell:** Martindale–Hubbell started in 1868 to help clients find a reliable attorney or law firm. Today, Martindale–Hubbell is a network that connects over one million attorneys to clients that need legal representation. Through this company, potential clients can investigate attorneys that they think would best represent them. One way is through their client review rating system. These reviews are given by people who have talked with the attorney or who hired the attorney or firm.[77] Martindale–Hubbell also provides peer reviews. Thus, feedback is not only from clients, but other attorneys and legal experts. This helps to give a well-rounded perspective of the potential attorney. With this system, you can know the genuine experiences of other clients or legal professionals in relation to the attorney you are considering.

2. **Super Lawyers:** The Super Lawyers directory provides clients in need of legal representation with profiles of experienced and qualified attorneys in their area. The Super Lawyers list offers attorneys that span a variety of practices of law as well as including attorneys from all over the country. To be part of Super Lawyers, attorneys must be

---

77 "About Martindale-Hubbell," Martindale-Avvo, accessed July 8, 2024, https://www.martindale.com/about-martindale-hubbell/.

recognized by peers in the field. Using Super Lawyers can help clients to narrow their search to make sure to find the right attorney for their case and situation, all while knowing that they are selecting a respected attorney.[78] However, the categories are very broad, and you will need to be sure that the attorney you selected actually has experience in the specific area you need.

3. **U.S. News & World Report—Law Firm Directory; Best Lawyers; Forbes:** U.S. News & World Report provides resources and information about more than five thousand law firms in America. Clients can use this directory to locate attorneys by state, city, or legal issue. This site is intended to help people locate attorneys who can help them with their specific legal needs.[79] Best Lawyers and Forbes are the newer attorney directories. All legal directories that you can't pay your way into are okay places to start your search.

4. **Avvo:** Founded in 2006, Avvo was started by an attorney who often received legal questions from friends. He realized there was a need for dependable legal advice—especially when it comes to choosing the right attorney. Avvo utilizes an algorithm that evaluates attorneys on a scale of 1 to 10. They also provide real reviews from various clients that have hired different attorneys and law firms. Additionally, Avvo connects clients with guidance in relation to their legal questions and needs. If clients aren't exactly sure what type of attorney they need for their legal matter, Avvo can help clients to discern what type of attorney connects best with their legal needs. After discovering what type of attorney

---

78 "Find Top Rated Lawyers in the U.S.," Super Lawyers, accessed July 8, 2024, https://attorneys.superlawyers.com/.

79 "U.S. News Law Firms," *U.S. News & World Report*, accessed July 8, 2024, https://law.usnews.com/law-firms#1.

best fits their needs, they can use Avvo to search for qualified and experienced attorneys in their area.[80]

5. **The National Trial Lawyers:** The National Trial Lawyers is an invitation-only organization of trial attorneys in the United States. Those that are part of this group go through a lengthy process, which includes peer reviews and research. Membership is only offered to a select few attorneys from each state. To be selected, the attorney must display strong leadership qualities, influence, reputation, and more. Thus, if you need a trial attorney in relation to personal injury or criminal matters, the National Trial Lawyers website is a wonderful place to locate experienced, reputable, and capable attorneys for your legal matter.[81] This is a good place to begin a search for a personal injury or commercial defense attorney.

6. **Lawdragon:** Lawdragon, founded in 2005, is a digital media company that provides helpful guides for attorneys and other legal content. Every year, Lawdragon publishes the guide 500 Leading Lawyers in America and offers a way to identify specific areas of practice for those attorneys. This is a good resource to locate experienced attorneys that can help you with your legal situation.[82] This is a good place to start a search.

There are separate groups that are practice-specific. For example, there are trial attorneys and associations, and other organizations that apply to specific areas of the law. You should research

---

80   "Find a Lawyer," Avvo, accessed July 8, 2024, https://www.avvo.com/find-a-lawyer.html.

81   "Member Directory," National Trial Lawyers, accessed July 8, 2024, https://thenationaltriallawyers.org/member-directory/.

82   "About Us," Lawdragon, accessed July 8, 2024, https://www.lawdragon.com/about.

the type of organizations that apply to the practice area you need and see if the attorney belongs to that organization. Better yet, see if the attorney is in a leadership position within the organization or has received awards from the organization.

Unfortunately, there are also groups that give out awards that do not have high standards or very good qualification screening processes. My wife, who is not an attorney, gets letters congratulating her on qualifications to some of these organizations. That is bad and harmful because a nonattorney won't necessarily know which groups are good and which ones are not. That is why I listed some of the more reliable ones earlier.

AWARDS

Check to see if the attorney that you are considering has received any awards that are applicable to the area of your legal concerns.

REVIEWS

We all use reviews when picking where to eat and what products to purchase. It is also a good idea to check out attorney reviews. Google reviews, Facebook reviews, Trustpilot, Better Business Bureau, and Yelp are some of the most popular review sources. Like any review process, you should look at the reviews to see if they are credible. I would be skeptical of those who have all five-star reviews and no lower reviews. I don't care how good you are; it is next to impossible to keep everyone perfectly happy. There are several ways that a business can pay for good reviews. I also know of some law firms that erase all reviews once they get bad. Suddenly, a two- or three-star review with hundreds of reviews gets deleted and the law firm suddenly starts over. So look at the number of reviews, the dates of the reviews, the comments (if any), and overall rankings.

INTERVIEW

It is important that you use the tools from this chapter to narrow the best of possible attorneys you would consider hiring to handle your case or legal matter. You should narrow your search to two or three different law firms or attorneys.

Once you have done your research and narrowed your search to two or three different highly skilled attorneys in the particular area you need, then you should schedule interviews with these attorneys. Good attorneys will be happy to be interviewed. The more complex and important the legal matter is, the more time you are likely to spend with that attorney or their staff.

I think the interview is the most important step in picking the best attorney for your needs. You should meet the attorney and everyone else who will be working on your case. You want to see if that attorney's personality is one that fits your personality. You should feel free to ask the attorney questions. If the attorney makes you feel uncomfortable, you know that is the wrong attorney for you. Below are some of the questions I would recommend:

1. Have you ever handled a case that is very similar to mine?
   A. If so, please provide details of this case.
2. How many attorneys will be working on my file, and how involved will you be in this case?
   A. Please explain the types of things each attorney will do.

3. Who else will be working on my case?
   A. Will there be paralegals?
4. (If it is litigation) When was the last time you went to trial, and what was the result?
   A. Do you regularly go to trial?
   B. If a case gets to trial, would you be the attorney handling the trial?
5. What is the cost associated with hiring the attorney? How will they be paid, and are there additional costs?
6. What are your office hours?
7. What if I have an issue or problem when your office isn't open?
8. How often will we meet to discuss my claims?
9. Who will be my primary contact?
10. Have you ever had a public or private reprimand or disciplinary action taken by the disciplinary committee of your state bar?
11. Have you ever been sued by a client for malpractice?
12. What percentage of your work is focused on the area of law that I need?
13. What awards have you received in the area of law that I need?
14. Have you written anything authoritative on the area of law I need?
15. Have you lectured or presented at legal conferences on the area of law that I need?
16. How well do you handle the expenses that are involved in handling my case?
17. (If it is a serious wrongful death, catastrophic injury, or semitruck wreck case) How soon will you hire experts, and what types of experts will you hire?

BAR ASSOCIATION AND OTHER
LEGAL ORGANIZATIONS

There are a variety of legal organizations or bar associations that an attorney can belong to. An attorney belonging to various organizations in a specific area of legal work is typically a good sign that the attorney is surrounding herself/himself with others in that area. A large group of peers to share knowledge or experience will enable the attorney to grow. So look for attorneys who belong to professional organizations. Also look for those that are in leadership positions in these areas.

Conclusion

ALTHOUGH IT HAS NEVER BEEN EASIER TO PICK THE wrong attorney, it has also never been easier to do the research to make sure that doesn't happen. Hopefully, this book helps you know how to pick the best attorney for your legal matter. Attorneys aren't all equal. The attorney you hire will have a lot to do with the outcome of your case. Be smart, do your research, ask the right questions, and pick an attorney who is experienced, knowledgeable, ethical, and a good fit for you or your family.

When you are faced with a major legal challenge, you want to hire the right attorney. Attorneys are not all equal. The wrong attorney can have devastating consequences for you and your family. Don't risk your future by picking an attorney because they are a good marketer. There are attorneys I would never hire who advertise heavily. There is also no correlation between being a good marketer and being a good lawyer. You deserve the best, and you shouldn't settle for the wrong attorney.

To hire the best attorney, you have to do your due diligence. You want an attorney who has significant experience in the specific legal issues you are dealing with. You want an attorney who has elite training and knowledge. You should start with board-certified attorneys who are ABA-approved by board-certified groups. After finding board-certified attorneys in your state, then you should do a Google search of these attorneys. Look for an attorney who teaches, writes, and lectures in the area you need. Check out the attorney's present memberships and awards. Look at their peer review rankings. Also look at their reviews and ratings from clients that can be found on places like Avvo and Google.

After narrowing your search to two or three attorneys who have the knowledge, training, and experience necessary to handle the specific legal issue you are facing, you should schedule interviews with these attorneys. Meet face-to-face to discuss their experience, results, and thoughts related to your case. Finally, you have done your due diligence, and you should be in a position to hire the right attorney.

Appendix I

HIRING THE BEST ATTORNEY TO HANDLE A SEMI WRECK CASE

In this book I answered the question of how to pick the right attorney and how to avoid picking the wrong attorney. Here I will use this information to give specifics on how to select the right attorney to handle a serious personal injury or wrongful death caused by a semi, heavy truck, or other commercial motor vehicle. These are the types of cases that I handle and have handled for over thirty-five years. I will show you how to use the knowledge I have shared to pick the right attorney. Regardless of the type of attorney you are picking, the process is the same.

A wreck involving a semi–tractor trailer, dump truck, flatbed, tanker truck, bus, or other commercial motor vehicle is not like other personal injury cases. A heavy truck accident case is not the same as a car accident case. There are many ways a truck wreck case is different than a car accident case. How those cases are investigated is different. The experts that are needed to prove your case are different. The law that applies is different. The standards are different. Insurance coverages are different. The investigation of other possible responsible parties is different. Negotiations are different. Mediations are different. Trial strategies are different.

The stakes are usually extremely high in these types of cases. When you or your family are the victims of a semi accident, you are often facing significant medical expenses, future medical expenses, loss of wages, loss of future earnings, life-care plans, pain, suffering, the loss of an enjoyment of life, or even worse—you may have had a family member killed in the wreck. The losses and damages can be extraordinary. It is more important than ever that you don't make a mistake and hire the wrong attorney. You must protect yourself and your family by doing what is necessary to pick the right attorney. Avoid picking an attorney because they are a good marketer on TV, buses, the radio, or internet ads. There are lawyers who will not be good at handling a semitruck wreck case. Pick an attorney who has the knowledge, experience, and resources to protect you and your family and to fight the trucking or insurance companies.

So you need to pick an attorney to handle your serious car accident with a semi. Possibly you have seen or been given the name of an attorney, but you don't know anything about them. Or perhaps you are starting from scratch. Regardless, the process is basically the same. Here is what I would recommend that you do to be sure you select the right attorney.

BOARD CERTIFICATION

There is a board certification in truck accident law. The National Board of Trial Advocacy is an ABA-accredited attorney certification program. They handle determining which attorneys are qualified to be board certified. Make sure that any attorney you are considering is board certified in truck accident law. This group knows what is necessary to handle these types of cases. They do a lot of the investigation and vetting for you. It is not easy to be board certified. It takes years of work in truck accident law to even attempt to be qualified. The attorney must have substantial experience. In addition, other attorneys, experts, and judges they have worked with, when handling semi cases, are questioned to be sure the attorney is qualified. The attorney also had to pass a test dealing with truck accident law.

By picking a board-certified attorney, you know you have an attorney who has the knowledge and experience to handle your case. At the time my book was written, there were only four attorneys in Indiana who had completed the certification process for truck accident law, and less than one hundred in the entire country. These attorneys were screened for you. Each of these attorneys had attorneys or judges who had seen the attorney in action and vouched for their expertise. They had to prove they had significant experience in the handling of these cases. A certain number of hours of experience was required for them to be on that list. In addition, they had to take an exam focused only on truck accident cases. They had to pass that test to get on that list.

Start by narrowing your search to a board-certified attorney in truck accident law. Next, look at the following suggestions.

MULTI-MILLION DOLLAR ADVOCATES FORUM

This is an organization that recognizes attorneys who have made multiple million-dollar recoveries for their client(s). Not all attorneys recover settlements or judgments in excess of $1 million. Some have never handled multimillion-dollar cases. If you have a significant case, you should have an attorney who has made significant recoveries. By selecting an attorney that has been recognized by this group, at least you know they have at least one substantial recovery for a client. Pick an attorney who has multimillion-dollar results.

SPEAKER, LECTURER, OR AUTHOR IN TRUCK ACCIDENT LAW

Attorneys who have written books, or chapters in books, on truck accidents demonstrate their expertise in the subject. Likewise, attorneys who speak, lecture, host podcasts, or are regular guests on podcasts that focus on large truck, semi, or commercial motor vehicle wrecks distinguish themselves and are worthy of your consideration. Pick an attorney who is actively educating others about truck wreck law.

MEMBER OF ATAA

The Academy of Truck Accident Attorneys is a premier group for attorneys handling commercial motor vehicle wreck cases. Although there are other good personal injury groups, none of them specialize or focus exclusively on semi, large truck, and other commercial motor vehicle accident cases. The ATAA is the only one. Pick an attorney who belongs to this group. You can go online and look for members in your state. By belonging to this group, the attorney has demonstrated a willingness to devote additional time to this area of law. You can also look to see if the attorney you are considering is on the Board of Regents in this group.

ETHICAL

You should check online with the discipline committee in the state where the attorney practices to be sure that the attorney is in good standing. I would suggest only choosing an attorney who has never been disciplined.

SUPER LAWYERS

Every state has a list of attorneys who have been peer-reviewed and selected as Super Lawyers in their state. Super Lawyers recognizes attorneys in different areas of the law. Look at the list and choose an attorney that has been selected as a Super Lawyer in personal injury plaintiff law. Even better is that Super Lawyers recognizes top-fifty and top-ten attorneys. Obviously, it is difficult to be included in the list of Super Lawyers, and even harder to be picked in the top-fifty or top-ten attorney lists. You should look for an attorney who has been selected for numerous years as a Super Lawyer in your state. It is even better if the one you are considering is in the top fifty or top ten.

MARTINDALE–HUBBELL

You should pick an attorney who has the highest ranking attainable with Martindale–Hubbell, known as an AV Preeminent rating. This rating demonstrates the highest level of professional excellence for their legal knowledge, communication skills, and the highest ethical standards. Pick an attorney with an AV Preeminent rating because they have been selected as the top of their field after the Martindale–Hubbell people checked with other attorneys in the same state about the attorney's skills, legal knowledge, and communication skills and verified that the attorney demonstrates the highest ethical standards.

AWARDS

Look for attorneys who have received awards for anything that relates to the practice of personal injury law. Specifically, look for awards in the truck accident area.

THE NATIONAL TRIAL LAWYERS—TOP 100 AND TOP 10 TRUCKING LAW

The National Trial Lawyers limits their groups to one hundred attorneys who practice personal injury law in each state. In addition, they have subgroups, such as truck accident law, that recognize only ten attorneys in a state. Pick an attorney who is recognized by this group in the area of truck accident law.

AAJ AND STATE TRIAL LAWYER GROUP

Look for an attorney who belongs to the American Association for Justice. This is a national group of plaintiff attorneys. By belonging to this group, the attorney has demonstrated a desire to learn and has been an advocate on behalf of personal injury clients and the safety of the public. Look for AAJ members who are also members of or have chaired the specified trucking subgroup. Also look for attorneys that are members of and active in state plaintiff trial lawyer groups. Again, this shows a desire to stay active and teach and learn.

REVIEWS

Choose an attorney who has a significant number of positive reviews. Reading what other clients have to say about an attorney that you are considering is extremely important. Check out their Google reviews or websites, Facebook reviews, and reviews on other sites.

INTERVIEW

This is one of the most important steps. You should interview any attorney that you are considering. Attorneys are all different, and it is important to make sure her/his personality is a good fit for you and your family. You will be spending a lot of time with this attorney and their office staff. It is important that you feel comfortable. I believe that the interview process is one of the most important steps in hiring the best attorney for your case.

Things to look for in an interview with an attorney:

1. How does the office look? Does it look run-down? A truck accident case takes a significant amount of money to prosecute. This is money that is advanced by your attorney. Your attorney must have the financial means to conduct the investigation and push your case to a resolution. By looking at the office, you may have a feel for the financial well-being of the attorney.
2. How are you treated by the receptionist and everyone else you come in contact with? Your case is a large case, and if people aren't treating you well in the beginning, then it's not likely that it will improve. It is more likely to get worse.
3. Is the attorney willing to answer your questions and encour-

aging you to ask all of your questions? Any good attorney is happy to answer your questions and won't make you feel bad for asking questions.

4. It is important that the attorney is willing to introduce you to everyone on the team. It takes more than one person to do a good job on a truck wreck case. You should know the entire team.

Assume that you have selected two or three attorneys who are AV-rated by Martindale–Hubbell; are Multi-Million Dollar Advocates Forum members, Super Lawyers, and board certified in truck accident law; have written or lectured on truck accident law; belong to the National Trial Lawyers; have received awards for their work; belong to the AAJ and state trial lawyer groups; are members of the ATAA; have no ethical complaints with the disciplinary commission; and have plenty of good Google or other reviews. Now you are ready to set up your interview. Here are some sample questions I would ask:

1. Have you handled similar cases? If so, how many?
   A. The attorney should describe the case and how it turned out.
2. Who is the team that will be working on the case, and what will everyone's role be?
   A. Insist on meeting the entire team.
3. What will the first steps be if I decide to hire you as my attorney?
   A. The attorney should be able to describe specific steps and experts she/he will have to preserve the evidence.
4. Have you ever tried a semitruck case? How often do you go to trial?
   A. Here it is important to discuss trial results. No one

wants to go to trial, but you want an attorney who the defense knows will go to trial if necessary. To get full value, the defense must believe that your attorney can force them to pay if necessary.

5. How do expenses and fees work?
   A. All personal injury agreements must be in writing. You should be given the agreement, and the attorney should answer all of your questions after the agreement.

6. Will you and your law firm handle the case if you think going to trial is necessary? Or will you refer it to another law firm?
   A. Some law firms never go to trial, and you deserve to know this in the beginning. Pick a firm that can go to trial even though you would prefer not to go to trial.

7. How quickly will you hire experts, and what types of experts will you hire?
   A. The attorney should be hiring experts right away on most cases. The types of experts that are hired include an accident reconstructionist and truck mechanics.

8. How do you handle the crash investigation?
   A. Our law firm has a crash response team, which includes an investigator. As soon as we are hired, we send the investigator to the scene and look for security cameras that might have captured the wreck. In addition, they track down the vehicles and look for evidence. Whomever you pick should be willing to start the investigation immediately.

9. Is an attorney involved in the vehicle inspection and download of the electronic data in the vehicle?
   A. Many good attorneys insist on being at the inspection and download. I have discovered things that would have been missed if I hadn't been there.

10. Which attorneys will be at the deposition?
   A. You want to be sure that the attorney taking the deposition of the truck driver, or representative for the trucking company, is an experienced truck accident attorney.
11. Do you or any of the other attorneys in your firm have a commercial driver's license? or Have you ever driven a semi?
   A. Certainly, hiring an attorney who is licensed to drive a semi or who has driven a semi is helpful and shows a higher level of dedication.
12. Do you use focus groups?
   A. The answer should be yes. If a case is of any significance, which these cases are, then the attorneys should regularly use focus groups. They should be able to discuss how they use focus groups.
13. Please describe how the case will proceed and how long it will take.
   A. Every case is different, but an experienced attorney should be able to give you a rough guideline on how your case will proceed.

Appendix II

QUALIFICATIONS	YES	NO
Board Certification		
Multi-Million Dollar Advocates Forum		
Speaker, Lecturer, or Author in Truck Accident Law		
Member of Academy of Truck Accident Attorneys (ATAA)		
Ethical (No ethical violations)		
Super Lawyers		
Martindale–Hubbell		
Awards		
The National Trial Lawyers—Top 100 and Top 10 Trucking Law		
American Association for Justice (AAJ) or State Trial Lawyers Groups		
Reviews		
Interview (Are they willing to be interviewed before being hired?)		

About the Authors

DAVID W. CRAIG is a nationally recognized trucking accident attorney with over thirty-five years of experience litigating catastrophic injury and wrongful death cases. He is board certified in truck accident law (2019 to present). David is a Trucking Top 10 Trial Lawyer and a Top 100 Trial Lawyer as designated by the National Trial Lawyers. He has an AV Pre-eminent rating (top rating) by Martindale–Hubbell. David has also been recognized as one of the top attorneys in Indiana by Super Lawyers and has risen to the top fifty.

David is a member of the Multi-Million Dollar and Million Dollar Advocates Forum. He has been chosen and named one of the Best Lawyers in America for personal injury litigation since 2017. He received the Thurgood Marshall Fighting for Justice Award from the Association of Plaintiff Interstate Trucking Lawyers of America. He is a Board of Regents member of the Association of Truck Accident Attorneys.

David hosts the podcast *After the Crash*, available everywhere you listen to podcasts. The video version is on YouTube. He is also the author of *Semitruck Wreck: A Guide for Victims and Their Families*, which is available on Amazon. He is a frequent presenter at attorney conferences and has chaired the Indiana Trial Lawyers Association Continuing Legal Education Seminar on Truck Accident Litigation.

David is married to Dana, and they have three children and several grandchildren. They live in Indianapolis, Indiana. When David is not working, he enjoys spending time with his family.

ABIGAIL HAYS has a passion for research, social justice, educating the public, and helping people to fight for their rights. Whether it is related to mental health, human trafficking, or hiring the best attorney for their legal matter, she firmly believes that people should have the right tools to help them make healthy and informed choices.

Abigail was born and raised in the state of Indiana, where she lives with her husband, Darin. She graduated summa cum laude in her undergraduate program and was chosen to be the commencement speaker at graduation. She then spent three years at a nonprofit working with survivors of sex trafficking and exploitation as well as educating fifth through twelfth graders about risks like abuse, trafficking, and predatory grooming. Abigail's work in these areas provides her with a unique perspective in relation to trauma, legal matters, and working with vulnerable populations.

Abigail will soon receive a master of social work degree from the Ohio State University. With this degree, Abigail hopes to provide trauma therapy. She enjoys lazy days reading a good book, hiking, sharing her faith, and spending time with her family.

www.ingramcontent.com/pod-product-compliance
Lightning Source LLC
Chambersburg PA
CBHW031903200326
41597CB00012B/523

9 781544 547640